INVISIBLE HORSES

ALSO BY PATRICIA GOEDICKE

Between Oceans
For the Four Corners
The Trail That Turns On Itself
The Dog That Was Barking Yesterday
Crossing the Same River
The King of Childhood
The Wind of Our Going
Listen, Love
The Tongues We Speak: New and Selected Poems
Paul Bunyan's Bearskin

INVISIBLE HORSES

PATRICIA GOEDICKE

MILKWEED EDITIONS

©1996, Text by Patricia Goedicke
All rights reserved. Except for brief quotations in critical articles or reviews,
no part of this book may be reproduced in any manner without prior written permission
from the publisher: Milkweed Editions, 430 First Avenue North, Suite 400,
Minneapolis, MN 55401
Distributed by Publishers Group West

Published 1996 by Milkweed Editions
Printed in the United States of America
Cover and interior designs by Tree Swenson
96 97 98 99 00 5 4 3 2 1
First Edition

Milkweed Editions is a not-for-profit publisher. We gratefully acknowledge support from the Bush Foundation; Target Stores, Dayton's, and Mervyn's by the Dayton Hudson Foundation; Ecolab Foundation; General Mills Foundation; Honeywell Foundation; Jerome Foundation; The McKnight Foundation; Andrew W. Mellon Foundation; Minnesota State Arts Board through an appropriation by the Minnesota State Legislature; Challenge and Literature Programs of the National Endowment for the Arts; The Lawrence and Elizabeth Ann O'Shaughnessy Charitable Income Trust in honor of Lawrence M. O'Shaughnessy; Piper Jaffray Companies, Inc.; The Ritz Foundation on behalf of Mr. and Mrs. E.J. Phelps Jr.; John and Beverly Rollwagen Fund of the Minneapolis Foundation; The St. Paul Companies, Inc.; Star Tribune/Cowles Media Foundation; Surdna Foundation; James R. Thorpe Foundation; Lila Wallace-Reader's Digest Literary Publishers Marketing Development Program, funded through a grant to the Council of Literary Magazines and Presses; and generous individuals.

Library of Congress Cataloging-in-Publication Data

Goedicke, Patricia.
    Invisible horses / Patricia Goedicke. — 1st ed.
    p. cm.
    ISBN 1-57131-403-2 (acid-free paper)
    I. Title.
  PS3557.032I58 1996
  811'.54—dc20   96-15040
                                                                                        CIP

This book is printed on acid-free paper.

CONTENTS

I. Uncharted   3

    Recipe   5
    Uncharted   7
    Stream   12
    In These Burning Stables   15
    As in a Cage   18
    The Three Tortoise Secret-of-the-World Power Plant   22
    Whirling Dervishes I   24
    Ideas   26
    The Jelly Between the Ears   28
    In This Landscape   31
    Ten Billion Blackbirds   34
    Because We Are Not Separate   37

II. Danger of Falling   41

    Precious Bodily Fluids   43
    Danger of Falling   47
    For Wiley, Age Six Months   50
    On the Porch   53
    What the Skin Knows   56
    Wild Card   58
    Cousins   59
    Stop the World   62

    Whirling Dervishes II   67
    In Bear Country   69

    The Gestures of Feeling   71
    The Word Float   75
    The Life of Each Seed   80
    Links/Talk Salad/Links   82
    Door/Ways   85
    These Words   90
    Under Cygnus   93
    Look, It's Poetry!   97

III. Baskets That Hold Nothing   105

    Before Dawn   107
    In the Skull's Tingling Auditorium   110
    Birds Like Basketball Players   114
    Because My Mother Was Deaf She Played the Piano   117
    Chase Scene, Many Levels   122
    Compose Yourself   125
    Treehouse   130
    Baskets That Hold Nothing   136
    From the Cliffs   138
    Directing Chapultepec Castle   141
    Lifeline   149

"It was said of [Richard Feynman, Nobel Prize Winning Physicist] that he had an extraordinary physical intuition, but that alone did not account for his analytic power. . . . 'As I'm talking,' he once said, 'I see vague pictures of Bessel functions from Jahnke and Emde's book, with light tan *j*'s, slightly violet-bluish *n*'s, and dark brown *x*'s flying around.'"
— JAMES GLEICK

"The words or the language, as they are written or spoken, do not seem to play any role in my mechanism of thought. The physical entities which seem to serve as elements in thought are certain signs and more or less clear images which can be 'voluntarily' reproduced and combined. . . . The above mentioned elements are, in my case, of visual and . . . muscular type."
— ALBERT EINSTEIN

FOR LEONARD:

Da capo al fine

INVISIBLE HORSES

I

UNCHARTED

"If I unfolded [the cerebral cortex] and laid it out on the table,
it would be the size of a large table napkin. And about as thick.
It would have ten billion neurons, at least—and a million
billion connections. If you counted the connections,
one per second, you'd finish counting them all
thirty-two million years later."
— Gerald Edelman

※

"For my part, when I enter most intimately into what I call *myself*,
I always stumble on some particular perception or other,
of heat or cold, light or shade, love or hatred, pain or pleasure.
I never can catch *myself* at any time without a perception,
and never can observe anything but the perception."
— David Hume

※

"We are the bees of the invisible. We wildly collect the honey of the
visible, to store it in the giant golden hive of the invisible."
— Rainer Maria Rilke

RECIPE

Each day the body puts on its pounds of tar.
Dark, viscous. Who can climb out of it?

One foot at a time. Lift. Fall back. Lift.

It is like dragging an iron bedstead behind you
all the way downstairs.

Try to shrug one shoulder without feeling it in the other.

The cargo in the hold shifts ominously,
the hull whistles and creaks.

Slow. Wallowing around in there with a few rubbery bones
and the brown spongy clumps of the pancreas, liver, etc.

Friends tug at the bars, make faces at you to come out.

But the flesh you live in is an anchor
of damp stones, you cannot move with or without it.

Rusty fluids pour, from one chamber
to another.

And you're stuck in them;
you'll never make it to the bridge.

How keep the head above waterline?

And the others in their own ships,
drowning.

Stick your nose out the hatch
and sail with the Big Dipper you can't,

The anchor won't let you.

One afternoon when your ears are ringing
in solitary

let go. Drop everything. Descend

like a diver into the vast
rustling folds of the ocean

and just hang there. Silent
as a pearl in an oyster but weightless,

revolving like a feather on its stem
or a thought.

It is like being a thought.

UNCHARTED

Water running, the low cough of it all night.

Below the threshold the river
mutters softly to itself, in the rumble

of deep cellos under bridges.

And you, drifting along in there, you whose inner
currents no one can touch

by daylight, up on the highways

that time you went for a walk, took a trip
and told no one, where did you think you were going?

~

Flashings only, the wet undersea flare
of one thought looming across another.

Hovering over you I lean
far out from the railings.

But the days revise themselves like wishbones,
voices telling their secrets to no one.

If I could wrap myself in the same sheets,
dive in there with you!

In the body's lonely laminations, its muffled
plates sliding and unsliding

as loons plunge, in watery corkscrews twisting,

who wouldn't want to descend
past who we say we are to the bottom?

And yet we can't, on the surface
skimming from meal to meal

all wells, all springs have buckets
save this one. And no windows, either;

only these rickety bridges, flimsy messages from one bank
to the other, with the water slipping through.

As day dissolves into day

even the spiral notebooks I fill
with inky scratches to keep count

from minute to minute disappear,

erase themselves from the mind's liquid
disintegrating pages.

Outside the house racketing
engines swoop the Interstate.

Next comes the news loop, the cool
gurgle of the latest lie . . .

No, never quite the same
thank God as the inner tides, the guttural

rising hormones, with their loose anchors drifting . . .

Across the continent trains snake
their black pearls, their glistening secret cargo

of drowned light from one coast to the next.

Wherever we look there are no berths, no words
to climb our way out of here,

But you, growling along by yourself,

whatever rapids race
predatory, through your bones,

whatever solitary pits open up in you

at the table, in the middle of conversation
without anyone's knowing,

hanging against the flow like a trout
or a chandelier, with diamond gills trembling,

inside you there's a whole city,
crowds breathing in your throat . . .

ༀ

And yet we live next door, and shake hands

in the morning, leaning on a bridge overlooking
the river together.

What is there to say but silence?

Staring into our lives
whatever observations we make are nothing

to these waters, uncharted.

Even love, carefully lowering itself into them,
never returns with the whole story but only drops,

one or two pailfuls at a time.

ༀ

Afterwards, bells moan,
warning buoys in the channel.

Up to our necks in moving
mouthfuls of black water

windmills churn, between the sweating cliffs

of the holy skin darting

pigeons weave, cloudlike
against a flowering sky.

Swimming below the world naked

ideas shift, cells press against the spine, rippling
tentatively onto the tongue

and then out, splashing into sight
but only in glimpses, what was that?

Minnow or bird swivelling,

wherever you're going I'm going
with you, pouring past each other in the ditches,

rushing along dark roads.

STREAM

    Finally it's your own
           private drinking fountain and you know it.
            With cool pillowing lips,
        whispers from yesterday's lovemaking,
      even the rasp of curses,
  as tag ends rise up
           in continually moist jets,
never mind the talk shows, the pseudo
    psychobabble battering at its captive
  crazed audiences locked in
          each evening to high
              glitzy commercials, ruthlessly ignorant
    cartoons trying to make us buy cars
        and politicians we don't need;
put you in solitary
      for years it's still there,
    in the cramped springhouse asking itself
        question after question, serious
  thrusts at the universe mixed
      with puns, tongue twisters, quips
        tossing their wild wet hair,
  with dim vowels, jokes
        murmuring quietly, lavender and chartreuse
video games talking to themselves in neon
      even when no one's using them,
    energy flashing like water
    trickling between roots
for nobody's particular
      benefit unless somebody happens
    to pay attention to it, but you carry

    the whole stream with you!
                      Awake or asleep it continues
    sometimes miserable, in heavy
        doldrums of aching regret
           the lost wife, the husband,
        the accident you ran away from, the one name
    you keep trying to forget;
even chained to the back of an immense
    dying turtle it keeps muttering,
    plates of submerged suffering
        can't keep it down, it simply
           cannot be muffled, little spurts of it,
    snatches of clothes, body parts, jingles
    pop up everywhere, *O Quiet!*
you want to yell at it but remember
        especially when you can't sleep,
           in sweaty pajamas twisting
    when nobody else is awake
    it's still there for you, sweetest
                out of the deepest
        desert aquifer, numbers
    and sheep to count, rhymes
    endlessly doing their tricks, in the circus
        that won't leave you, in the damp
    secret glittering at the center
just listen to it, mumbling
        and glimmering away inside there,
           keeping itself company
    below the flickering, blurred
        face of the digital clock,

inside as well as outside,
            with the water down to a thin ribbon
    all night, in the constant
    lonely click of a traffic light
        addressing empty streets,
even with no cars on them it keeps going
    as long as you do,
no wonder sometimes you think you could drink from it
        forever and not stop

IN THESE BURNING STABLES

And yet you can't catch them. Even peering inside
as hard as you can, stumbling around in this hodgepodge

of jolts, shivers. Enzymes digesting themselves, muscles
relaxed or jerking,

head keeping time, noticing and not noticing
each whirr of the clock

especially when it stops.
But whenever you try to look for them

it's like mayflies swarming; in the thronged

brief hustle of the mind what are these transparent
puffs of air, ideas forming out of nowhere?

Battalions of tiny hooves. In thin sheets trampling,
sweeping across the cortex. Like leaves whipped by the wind

they keep disappearing, like the deep cherrywood sound
of the piano you heard last night. Or the vanishing

muffled oranges of sunset, the color
of peaches inside a refrigerator, the wash of chocolaty gray

silks no one has ever seen, none of them touchable.

The neurosurgeon can't know what you're thinking
until you tell him, but already it's too late,

the long faces of thought slide
into each other like layers of purple and brown oil

in a portrait by Rembrandt, muffled
dim highlights drift

like berries in the woods, pieces of cottonwood fluff.

With no warning, suddenly
you come upon them in clusters,

little gusts leap up
like grasshoppers, all around you

from second to second changing, but watching over it,
who knows when, exactly, water will decide to boil

or wood finally ignite, or how,
precisely, ideas take shape, materialize, open the gates?

Whiff of stallion on the air.

The hair on the back of your neck bristles
where you can't see it, fire

where there's no fire but the taste of it,

ozone sizzling in the mouth
like a memory but what is that?

Invisible horses churn
like roiled smoke in the corral.

You try to lead them out
with the halter of the word *like*,

but even with the tiniest stitches, the most delicate
intracerebral loops

there's no lassoing them; in these burning stables
silhouetted against the flames

with calm eyes, with magnificent
tall shoulders, shadowy

gigantic haunches pass
and repass each other in the dark.

AS IN A CAGE

      Closed, most faces. The bleak, waiting   look
      of them.   Tight, wild-eyed
      as monkeys,   when one goes by

      sometimes, in a crowd   coming out of the movies
      suddenly one's staring   straight at us
      dark knot,   convulsed

      clenched around some   white fist, bone of longing
      what is it that cannot   be spoken of
      without letting on   how   ignorant we are

      as in a cage   confined
      with the blue smell of breath,
      roar of gas in the stomach,   we are more

      than we know,   the inner organs press   hotly
      mold us into shapes   we cannot see:
      pistons thud   contracting diaphragms   squeeze

      the whole damp   engine sends out its signals
      and receives them
      but with no music   only static

      shut up here in our own   narrow grooves
      with squeaks, groans, hisses   whiskery mouse raspings
      we try to get out,   what if I

serenaded you,   would you
let me come in?   Because it's so dangerous, breaking
and entering.   Dry coughs, coiled

cigarette smoke leaks out
through the clapboards of the house   next door
where the two old ladies quaver

like me, after only a squirrel's
quick scurry on the roof,   *who's there?*
Opening our doors to nothing

but known evils   robber
doctors that crawl out from under   lowering intestines
like mechanics   wiping their foreheads

with soiled gloves   not seeing
anything but the meat   of the walnut
digging at it

behind the grillwork   cramped
there's no harmony   only snarls,
aching cavities filled

with fine tendrils waving
from one battery to the next   reaching
out for each other but the spark plugs

keep missing   if you won't let me
or I you,   watching late night television
slumped over the remote   control buttons

*

what can we know firsthand,   following
the game shows   imagining giving the right answer
is the right answer, peering

at shadows behind glass   or *in vitro,* safely
computerized amoebic squiggles   the inviolable golden glow
of prime numbers   color-enhanced islands

in random clumps,   patterns
we recognize but can't quite   unlock
what if the key   really is music

with its secret combinations,   wordless
flutes pearling,   ladders of sound, languages
like looped wings   unfolding

over drummed growls asking   then answering themselves
in double choruses, canons   with no conductor, soaring
only to unravel

and start again, what some of us perform
others listen to,   trying to understand
the connection,   in here with the monkeys

matter making its own music   everywhere,   without us
all these complicated notes,
coded chromosomes ringing

their own changes,   from sheet to tiny sheet
whole species talking to each other in tongues
we were born with but can barely   speak.

THE THREE TORTOISE
SECRET-OF-THE-WORLD POWER PLANT

At the exact center of the invisible
               cold, choppy, out-to-the-horizon expanse
     of a wild ocean inside everyone, mysterious
          fins drifting across it,
       what would this giant, this rainwater polished
   shimmering sculpted block
              of marbled whiteness be?

Perhaps it is a sperm whale
           or a solitary godhead, ticking.
Occasionally a black crow flaps over it,
              starfish-footed, catches its
       angry balance on the edge,
   but mostly we pay no attention to it,
             shopping, sharpening pencils
     somehow we almost forget but we can't:
eons ago it was mute,
     solid from ear to ear but today,
   chewing its underwater lips like a full moon caught in a trap,
      it talks softly to itself:
           What split us in two
   in the first place, what cracked
        the ripe halves of the melon
     apart from themselves and why?

Once we floated along
         in perfect comfort: domed, beautiful,
    ignorant but all-of-a-piece,
      but now we're divided, there's something else, inside:

      though the body's free to live
         better than ever before,
   as the mind materializes itself
         and all of its theories on the broad backs
of the Three Tortoise Secret-of-the-World Power Plant,
what created it, and who, and where did it come from
   we still don't know, on the deck of a dying submarine
         subtly fractured, immense
     as a pale iceberg, looming, glacially wrinkled,
           has anyone ever walked around it
     twice, and come out alive?

Brain surgeons, testing its wires,
     nervous as pecking birds skitter
   over its narrow cracks leaping
      from one tiny vein to another asking
Rivers, where do you go
        when the light's off?
       Up from the forehead breathing
          feathery plumes rise
       beside every highway, chill
    halos of ghostly air
   strange as motel ice makers
       on the hottest July day, the least
crystallization of power as amazing
     as the greatest, hidden machines
   making the desert bearable
        even as they dwindle away.

WHIRLING DERVISHES I

and there's no resting from it,
all of us walking around holding up these
agitated beehives, spinning
tornadoes of energy, cyclones
of peppery specks popping
on top of our necks, even on the subway, watch out,
don't bump into them! delicate skulls bobble
as the train jolts to a halt, pyramids of gray
or is it pink clouds of brain matter lurch, twist
like bowls of ocean sloshing

without even a leak, imagine
all that electricity fizzing
and nobody gets hurt by it, struck by lightning
or even shocked, usually: low voltage for such high
performance, in long lines jazzing out to the
whole world to manage it, build rockets and skyscrapers,
invent the Internet, communicate
intelligently with each other but however gently

you tap the keys be careful, how did you do it,
raise even a finger
without thinking about it or *was* that thinking
without your noticing? each day you buy a newspaper
for the train ride, fold it carefully, read it
and then digest it but how,
what are those bees doing in there, can anyone see them,
taste them, touch them, who's that talking to you and when,
exactly, did chemicals learn to speak? well

they didn't, actually, but then what's
happening, from one jittering dendrite
to another, it's too fast,
your head's beginning to ache
just trying to imagine it. so, sit down
on the seat, take a load off
your mind or is it your feet?

even when you're asleep
there's no controlling them, the nightmares
or the daydreams either, what was that in the paper about Clinton
and the stock market that started you chasing the volleyball
at Green Harbor with your brothers,
what new engrams are these, spinning and twirling

bits and pieces of short-term
or is it long-term memory whizzing by
like twigs, like the dots and dashes
of what uncrackable code leapfrogging
and whirling around in there
with the bees?

IDEAS

    The thin bars of the traps
                we let down day by day
       to catch gossiping lobsters for mere
                table talk or the deep, ongoing
    history of the sea's long
                affair with earth and where we stand on it
    and how, all the clever cat's cradles
                we weave for ourselves shudder
       at every passing barracuda. Each explanation
we invent shines fitfully
                but proudly
    against the reefs it grows from

and wants to make love to,
                illuminate even those dark
    seething carpets of other, wilder
                hungrier scholars that seem almost
to swallow us. In rippling schools. Masses
    of small bottom fish,
                corpuscles oozing into thick
    crusted plaques, the seep of cells
                wormlike, secretly dividing
    and then multiplying into live
clumped coral. Buzzing. With eager
                electric hooks, pronged feet, tiny
    red starfish hanging all over

the fringed eyehole we peer through, what
                ceaseless activity! Would they tear us

                    apart?
            No. They are too blind—
                too random for that. But both kinds
            of colonists urgently need
                each other, every answer
                        comes caked with the prickly
            slime of barnacles, the
                    cages we think we've erected
                        against sharks and other predators are frail
                            ghost crabs, their near see-through
                    slats sway in the hissing crackle
        of the cold soup that created them.

THE JELLY BETWEEN THE EARS

sparkles in its cup. Jiggles. Imaginary giant waves,
tiny sugars and salts flicker against each other,
sweep back and forth, protected
as milk in a bowl:
                    yes, but
not for long. Flattening, over the years
like the rubber heel of an
old shoe.
          Or bubble gum, or a nearly worn-down
eraser: what does it erase, itself?
The jelly between the ears
hardening.
          But still soft to the touch, the
toes find their own nooks. Nuzzle into them
as before, a
          few lights bobbing
low down on the interior concourse.

Flights from Africa. Mars. Memory jets
that keep arriving and departing
sometimes on command, sometimes
not.
          Engines sputter and twist
back on themselves. In old grooves,
patterns burned into a computer.
                            Synapses
freeze in their tracks. Refuse to fire or won't stop
stuttering, repeating themselves like rifles:
                                let me tell you
the story I told you yesterday: how

boring. Except for one or two red-hot
hollering matches,
     chances to warm up
the old arteries with a few shots
of adrenalin,
    lob a couple of Hawkeye
missiles into the breakfast nook, the IQ
testing lab, the country next door, why not?
             Each one of us
stumble-footed, heading the same direction
into the ground.
     Like lumps in a saucepan, stiffening
clumps of selfishness. Raw, glistening
knobs stuck in the cracked
leather of the head's
shoe pot.

     So, what should we listen to,
the young before they harden? Inside
clever spelunkers with their lamps
must come.
     The ghost you thought was yours
exhales itself into cinders,
evaporates up the smokestack.
          Each brain
melts into earth's stews. Slides, then crawls
out of the steam into new
species never tasted.

Ugly? Worse than before? Too long coagulated
in here without knowing. The slow ooze of matter

stops up all the exits.

With dwarf hummocks. Baby booties
cast in bronze. Where did I put
my last idea?
                      The moths are everywhere,
eating. The guns of the world cough up
the thick phlegm, the choked rattle of the dying.
                                  Over the slumped acres of the dead
what does it matter? Outside all the cities
there are sacks of forgetfulness heaped up,
lost shoes scattered among the graveyards.
                                            After the battle the scavengers:
at midnight, one or two stray children, curious.
With their brand-new flashlights.

IN THIS LANDSCAPE

With everything squashed together,
                outside the window tangled
         brown branches with cotton in their arms,
                  with one large foot in its fur
            leather slipper curled
                    next to the portable radio perched
              on the arm of the chair like some perky
    little black bird singing Stravinsky,

with all those slippery
            suave oboes, warbled
        smooth strings sliding into the yellow shag rug
           studded all over with paper clips,
              lost straight pins, ambushed
        flat shiny flecks
            of pointillist paint,

  if nothing stands by itself
              in this mustard-colored field,
      if each blade brushes against the next
          in dusty impasto crushed up
         into the nose like some thick
      motionless soup, if the layers
         are so crowded how is it possible to move,
    stick up a single hand
        outside the juicy glue of the present, the

frame that contains us, in this one
                  molecular composition that keeps everyone's
      feet planted, bottoms firmly supported
           by plump chairs,

        tender heads by apparently
    solid pillows, perceptions that hold us together

even as they keep us apart;
        though you want to extend your arms,
       gather the whole world into them you can't
   get there from here, as the neighbor's
     house across the street flattens itself
         against your window, without perspective there's no

way to stand back, hold anything
    close to you, in dense brush strokes distinctions
          like clogged pores congeal
    in lush blobs of pure matter trapped
  so heavily it seems impossible to get out but of course you do,
    in the lens of the mind's eye, in books
      opening and closing, taking thought
    all sticky daubs dissolve:

imperceptibly your left wrist,
      the one you're leaning on, its bright
        gold hairs begin to bleed
          into the grassblade rug, out the door
   and downstairs like a dog set free, trotting
      suddenly off to the mountains!

Fifty miles away they rise straight up
    out of the valley bearing their white-ridged grandeur
        north to Canada,
    the air of your head fills
      with eagles, far-off

          clumps of snow falling
    from green branches, the quiet
              of chill water over stones
        you can't possibly step on but you do
    whenever you happen to think of them;

then there's what's going on
      right now, in the jazz band of your ears,
    from the high-pitched ringing in them to the queer
            rasp of your breath to the downstairs'
      familiar rumbles, thumps, creaks,
the next thing you do is listen

for someone, anyone: child, friend, husband
          moving around down there in the kitchen;
    so what if you've only drawn him in
        to suit yourself?
     Because what gives any of us
       substance at all is the belief, however sketchy
           in some source of light
        however hidden, that there's at least
     something outside

Or maybe inside, propped up against the wall,
    there he still is, by the refrigerator,
        mysterious as a figure painted
in the corner of a canvas, beneath trees
         —for perspective's sake only?—
     maybe even listening to Stravinsky
   himself, over a glass of milk,
       thinking his own thoughts.

TEN BILLION BLACKBIRDS

But slowly, with all that glittering
intelligence beginning to cloud over,

shadows plunge their long fingers
everywhere into your thinking.

So you insist, but what tricks
you still play on us!

Trills, perfect
thrush music from the bushes.

Who cares about a few
lost keys, connections

missed?

As if anyone could contain
all of you.

Not to mention the attached

body. Legs dangling. Miles
and miles of arterial highways, the

head, the heavy head
on its trunk,

boughs humming with the complicated

high-speed intercellular
exchanges of ten billion

tiny blackbirds packed into one square millimeter
of branching brain matter and jiggling

yes, jiggling. Though the pie's shrinking, for all of us
everywhere into crumbs, vaguely remembered

names, faces, a nursery rhyme or two,

the mystery of it's still trembling
beneath each crusted skull

and you know it:

in the battering raids of gap-toothed
scattershot absences,

crows falling from a brain sky
full of holes

you keep after them,
in the mind's archipelagoes wandering

even among towering waves

you can't be toppled,
with the rest of us you escape

from atoll to distant atoll:

as gannets on the ocean sleeping
at the slightest touch rise up

ring after fluttering ring

the engines that power us wait only
to be discovered, axons and dendrites rustling

inside everyone, billions and billions of them
shaking their tiny wings.

BECAUSE WE ARE NOT SEPARATE

On the calm bed waking
        uneasily, confused by the blurred lines
   between the center and the outer edges,
      with no one beside us, with hearts suddenly speeding
           like cars on the beltways, with the hot
       breath of exhaust on our necks, frantic
as crabs scuttling for cover,
    with the sea drawn back from its margins
        retreating, leaving its brittle frill on the beach,
   no wonder there's nothing left to believe in,
        not permanently

※

except behind the eyelids drifting.
          Idle as dust motes, quiet
     deep down in the darkness
   where everyone lives, hidden
           in the blessed secular smoothness
every once in awhile of no crime, no criminal,
      first to return is the skin, exquisite
as a hummingbird, the swift kick of its
         wiry claws flickering
   almost too fast, but slow down,
     here are the legs, just feel them,

※

in the empty rain barrel what has hardened,
    over the years been squeezed dry, tossed in a waterless corner

     is blossoming now, unfurling itself like a sponge,
    as white sheets slip along the calves
       like a cool breeze, iridescent,
   the foot like a leaf flexes
     and then relaxes, such lightness
you can't help but trust it,
   floating in your bones
  with nothing to weigh you down,
     connected
      to the hairbrush on the floor, to the humming power lines
outside the window there is sunlight, there is water
   and bittersweet cries

       🍃

for in spite of the harsh traffic,
     the bleeding houses, the poison
    polluting the cities or because of it, who knows,
     because we are not separate,
  by merest accident, some mornings it really seems possible
     to join all our edges:
   with luck and a long sigh moving
      soft, wild, familiar as a wet flower,
   gardenia pearled in its leaves,
the self that is no self contracts and then expands,
   the boat that is no boat takes over

       🍃

as the ship that contains nothing disappears
        far back in the head, it sinks below the horizon
           to a sea full of tiny strangers
   who are not strangers,
               deep as the world is small
     among gray land masses, vague floaters moving
  lazily, here in the shy dark
          of our own pillows, pieces of all we have ever met
  or not met, easy as feathers come sailing
            into each exquisite pore of the skin,
      entire oceans going out
and then returning, meeting themselves coming back in.

II

DANGER OF FALLING

"The naïve boundary between 'me' and 'the outside world' is my skin (and the lenses of my eyes) but, as we learn more and more about the way events in our own bodies can be inaccessible to 'us,' the great outside encroaches."
—Daniel Dennett

"You say 'I' and you are proud of this word. But greater than this—although you will not believe in it—is your body and its great intelligence, which does not say 'I' but performs 'I'."
—Friedrich Nietzsche

"The deep texture of everyday language is dualistic. . . . The dying patient says, 'This can't be happening to *me*.' Because the mind is clear: 'Why is my body letting *me* down?'"
—Gerald Edelman

PRECIOUS BODILY FLUIDS

Like semen, they told us. A joke
was it? Strange
currents slide through the interior channels.

And then I was given a wound
that wouldn't stop draining. The little plastic pouch
hung on my side like a monkey. To catch the lymphatic

secretions. Slowly it filled up, all day
plumper and plumper until it was pale cherry colored,
one third watery red, the rest glistening

transparent apricot. Dilute orange and
cranberry juice, I thought, gagging
on rows of paper dollcups Safeway had set out

for thirsty shoppers.
And came home and unplugged the stopper
three times a day, measuring it out carefully

before I emptied it, the ambient gingerale
of all those tiny tides coming and going
that keep our beaches clean.

The physicians insist it's nothing, a small drop in the level,
but maimed, aging here like a lopsided
slightly shivering fish, I speak from inside

the aquarium: what if I still need it
to swim in, how would they know
the true wetness of the undercurrents

of anyone else's ocean?
Unless it's contained, held in the sweet cups
of the body and nowhere else, it's dead

almost immediately on arrival;
inside here we're safe
but so lonely: sloshing around in our own

flooding liquids, who knows what's going on
beneath the skin, in the pale syrup that flushes us
from toe to fingertip? From mute, involuntary muscle

to the noisiest speech center, there where neurons twitch
and spit at each other like popguns, bits of matter
like sticks trailing their legs behind them,

calm sentences with complex, lazy
cellular faces float by without my
even asking, garbled voices murmur

in all our heads but who hears them, sometimes
there are flashes we almost know, entire phrases
shine at us from the top of a wave

just as it breaks off. Crashes down on the rock
of the need for a cigarette. Or a kiss,
some shadowy urge brushes across the face

and then it's gone. But caught in the undertow, we keep trying
to hold up our heads, hurl ourselves onto
paper rafts. With ink for ropes. Because what if

something's singing in here?
The lymph's lemony champagne soothes. Heals.
As undersea pebbles crackle

in the echoing caves of the blood, my God the blood,
don't lose it. Give it away, watch the strawberry column rise
in the hospital needle but don't let it pour out

too freely: it's too dangerous
and too powerful, carrying all its precise, ribboned
messages in its arms, more precious

than the yellow stream of urine
when it finally comes, it's the odor of moist earth,
ozone on an outdoor jacket. Crisp particles

of lymph spray the bathroom with the wild
piny aroma of nail polish. Banana. Peach. Intoxicating
sap of the world. How purely

fragrant we are. The scent of life's velvet
and clean: hidden tributaries crisscrossed
all over with the skitter

of waterbugs explaining themselves to each other
without words, with no one
inside here but ourselves, how can we help it,

with sighs, with fingers feathering,
with hungry gasps we tug at each other's
taut bodies, desperate

to open the gates, but once we rush outside
we're beyond saving; all that eloquent
gushing energy spends itself

like stale seawater:
as the liquid secret shrivels and dries up
into sticky specks scribbled

on skin or crumpled handkerchief, no more than mother's
spilled milk, no more than the sour
baptismal trickle of colostrum,

no more than the rough jostle and squirt,
the white, messy explosion into glass womb
or urgent hand does its life in air matter.

DANGER OF FALLING

The way calcium grows

all by itself into bone, microscopic
fraction attaches itself to fraction

or clouds crystallize, or blizzards congeal into hard
ice on aluminum wings,

even the astronauts' bodysuits can't cover up
the sheer strangeness of it, the extraordinary being-here

or anywhere, the skin of the plane could easily peel back
like an ear of corn and then what's to be seen but *who, me?*

the live, disintegrating,
terrified Barbie Doll asks, stuffed into her jeans

like a stick of butter, her neat, pointed feet dangerously
stuck into sky . . .

but still, teetering down the aisle
if anyone bumps her she glares, *This Is My Territory,*

this little packet of a hundred and twenty-two
pounds more or less says *Move it, Babe,*

one minute the cold kitchen, next minute Miami Beach,
digging into the sand beside the violent-

ly green sea, droplets of Almighty coconut oil
under the crisp tang of salt drizzle and lick

all over its bare, lusciously bronzed congregation
of too too solid—

No! Never in this world, the greedy molecules hiss

as the plane turns inland, the woman returns to her seat
past all the other anonymous collections of cells,

some snoring, some fussing with their kids,
one bent over a laptop, another staring

straight at her for a second, with X-ray
exhausted eyes peering, then swiveling away

as if they'd known each other before, fellow crew members
from another planet,

though the woman thinks of herself only on Main Street—my
my what an arrangement of chromosomes collected

who knows why—up here among streaked, boiling clouds
with the plane speeding through them, how

unexpected it is, how far the body travels
from its babyhood, locked in its charged circuits

she thinks about edges, the leathery sunburned skin
flaking off, in filmy shreds,

sound barriers breaking away from her but here she still is
for this one second fixed, eyes sticking out of the top of her face

like the glint of a buried pin or the beak
of a mother robin in the nest

she made for herself:

with earth losing its outer walls
twig by twig, what is this naked fork quivering

in the middle of Whose consciousness

she keeps wondering, whizzing across the face
of an electric cloud chamber,

here all I am
is falling, in the tight ship of the diminished,

in hot chips of pure
ignorant energy fizzing around some magnet,

some lucky iron only
imagination can count on,

trembling, gritting her teeth on the thread
of an end she can't know,

*Please, Someone, materialize me
in arms I can love always*

she whispers to herself,
Beam Me Up . . .

FOR WILEY, AGE SIX MONTHS

    Over his mother's shoulder Wiley
            age six months, trains his blue
  tracer-bullet eyes, merry
          round mystical stare
     right *at* me, follows my
             slightest move, coos

but keeps watching me as if I were
            a dog, a leaf, something
  real as the paper mobile above his crib
  —*me!*—
and all my insecurities just
       hanging there

for Wiley's pleasure alone,
        almost as if I had no
  other existence, no
           obsessive worries about mean
      crows' feet, jowls
    under my chin, wondering
     always about illusion, who
or even *if* I am, what on earth does it matter

to Wiley, anyway, in order
     to grow, not to disappear
entirely into speculation, the nature
        of the experiment's the same
    always, at any particular moment
   probably all I am is a moving
      shifting object to be grabbed,

    licked, sucked at, no more
                nor less interesting
        than his mother's breast, that
              absolute other we become
    despite ourselves,
        of, *for* everyone,

friends, neighbors, dinners
              to be microwaved, hair
        and lawns to be barbered, whatever
    drags us into some sense
            of solid self *felt*

if not always by ourselves, at least
        occasionally, enough to be fed upon
            by others, each one of us the world's
oyster, however small, guerrilla
            armies of mosquitoes, ants
march across my foot even as I look up

at the seashore,
        right outside the motel, in a rainstorm
            on a manicured strip of grass
  a gang of seagulls squats
                like thugs braced against the wind
        in tight formation, all facing

the same way, with mussed
        scrawny feathers hunched, teetering
    on the balls of their spiked feet,

scowling at the wet like dwarf
    secret police, football players aimed
        right *at* me, gleaming at me
like eyes whenever I look up
        suddenly.

ON THE PORCH

It's so quiet it's almost frightening; in the tawny
biscuit color of evening, great green

leaf clusters lean in at us, a windchime
across the street speaks up

a blue scale and down. A child goes by
on a bicycle, whizzing. Then two students

in sneakers, nudging each other.

But here we are nearly immobile. Huge mattresses
of silence slide out under our bodies

and lift us, and float us across the lawn
as if we'd been hollowed out, drawn

into thin filaments of ourselves,
vague faces listening

like blurred antennae quivering . . .

At nine o'clock, ten o'clock, it's still bright
and slightly menacing: a fast car

suddenly whisks by

as Sentinel Hill looks down
over its shoulders at the shadows beginning to slip

between houses: in the mild
lion light of summer

on porches all over town

the people next door pop in and out
unexpectedly, they run errands

all day long but now nothing, after a quick

juicy giggle, the slow dying-away fall
of a low voice on the corner, some stranger

saying good night, the quietness
spreads out everywhere, when everyone disappears

in summer, after work
where do they go?

Sitting quietly on their porches

or asleep, no longer present
any more than the leaves bowing

and nodding absently to each other,

for all the brain's endless
intercellular whisperings,

strands of protein rustling
and waving back and forth like wheat,

the mind in its windy armchair murmuring
barely believes in itself:

as slow water drops
from the dark lavender petunias

in their K Mart pot above us,

high overhead, in the black backyards of space,
cerebral circuits flash

and babble to themselves, lonely

as far-off satellites, blind sparks blinking,
signalling across the night.

WHAT THE SKIN KNOWS

the underside of one wrist
says to the other.

Peeled green
and white

what swims across the bridge
is tiny

tinier than diamonds

slick as the gleam of wet
new eggs

traveling along a stick.

Flesh crackles to confess
what lies within

body unsheathed
open

fingertips on fire
cool as rivers

the desolate flames of saints
flicker around the buttocks

tongues curl into ears

ivy sticks to the cathedral
digs in

with its little feet
creeps between the cracks

glistening

is that a tear beaded
on the eyelash?

We who have come so far
inside

where has it gone

the bird flies so fast
from one window to the other

what the skin knows
it forgets

WILD CARD

The leaves again. And the wind
shuffling through them, pack upon pack of wild

green playing cards, fistfuls of forest swooping
and churning through the air.

Or doves in a flurry. Or green shoals
of fish darting and shooting.

Let me shake out my hair. Let it tumble.
Like waterfalls. Crazed fireflies in a field.

And let you listen to the blood:
its linked cells beating.

Where is the luck we need?
Or where is the trunk of the tree?

The ant reaches for it,
the milkweed pod fluffs out.

Waves crash on a beach.

As packs of tuna leap up, surge over the barrier
their mouths are filled with leaves. And mine with wild

windy cries. There is no membrane between us.
Let the scales fall from our eyes.

COUSINS

High. Mindless. Cackle at the edge of the world.
And the geese are flying there

and crying, for two weeks now they've come racketing
each morning, miles and miles of them, pouring.

Where do they come from, where did they sleep
last night?

I can't see them, but the question chirrs like a clock

about to strike. In the East there are golf courses, soft beds
where they can fatten and die.

But here there are only prairies. Stubbled
hay fields. And a few marshes.

Sluggish, with wet trickles,
snakes twisting where the geese rest

until they can rise again, into cold
scurrying clouds rattling. The mad yammer

and rasp of them is a zipper,
a sewing machine clacking.

As if anyone could interpret

the sounds they make, which are nasal. Long and
narrow.

Something is weaving through the blood

we don't know. Right now, the radio
in my head switches channels: the latest flu virus

from Asia crosses the ocean, with heads crammed
in the dank holds of barges, in the stuffy cabins

of superjets, microbes riding the tall air
over our heads to Montana, where the geese clamor

like hounds baying after ghosts. Like confused hunters
with rifles chattering, doubling back on themselves, where are we

and where are we going? In the East,
nowhere. Stopped dead. On green fairways

nesting all year among golf balls.

In the Midwest the subdivisions multiply
so fast over their feeding places

finally the state of Minnesota heaps them all up

into Boeing 747s heading South, airlifted
over their own flyways.

Now, listening to them babble

out there on the horizon, ribboning along the crack
between earth and sky undulating

like oiled rivers, endless
as the coils of a Greek meander,

what's lost is among us,
streaming along the arteries and the bones

of gazelles. Polar bears. Spiders.
Porpoises wallowing in nets, sweet chlorophyll

in autumn abandoning the trees, the crisp scarlet molecules
brittle now, and dying, what if they don't

ever come back? Mad, frantic-seeming

as carnival barkers, each year with these families
in their ragged echelons, I can't tell

what they're saying but I feel them

like brothers and sisters, each following the same
or almost the same secret instructions for flying

as I do, cousins calling to each other
to stick together, but even as we cry out

from cold marshes, from fertile estuaries flooding
into grainfields and even golf courses, from the far reaches

of the Arctic tundra, out of the darkness honking

the geese are going now, in the pre-dawn
mists of origin they flow over us and beyond.

STOP THE WORLD

The way things move when they're not moving. Sickening, the
lurch of consciousness when you find out
at the railroad station suddenly the train

right next to you's leaving,
good-bye to the man twirling his dreadlocks,
the woman fingering her tattoo, the boy with the long neck,
eyes closed, Adam's apple wobbling . . .

But even if it's you leaving them, down the track as planned,
carefully following each step of the argument,
even when you're certain
you're in control at last, often you look up

from your car and all at once the traffic's moving
around you, the stoplight's changed
without your noticing or has it? Mouths opening and closing

behind closed windows, confident, each one
on the carphone earnestly explaining who started it
and why, calmly we keep inventing ourselves

in the rearview mirror, the one face we think won't move
away from us ever: central, composed, fixed
but still capable of frightening, sometimes the mask comes unglued,

for a second you can't tell, is that a stranger
wearing your hairdo or isn't it? With asterisk eyes jiggling,
with the sly gills of a minnow

trembling in the glass, telling you strange stories
you never knew you knew, what's going on
in your own head, where did these squiggles drifting

over the water like specks of fish food come from
in the first place, who bit your tongue?
Last night someone in your sleep was grinding

your teeth, who was it? Small animals, growling.
You try to hold onto the self
you think is yours. But now leg cramps wake you

so violently you can't help it, feet jerking like a dog
wild with fleas, skin twitching, worrying each itch
in blind spasms, next you catch yourself snoring, nasty

rattle. Wheeze. Catch. And try to stop it but can't:
suddenly you're falling, who
or what pushed you? Sex surely can't be all of it,

can it? Armies of cells rushing back and forth
in the hot bed of the brain probably overexcite themselves
fairly often but there are other motions,

nerves jumping and buzzing, kidneys going about their business
quietly: as poisons sink into the liver and cleanse themselves
the blood comes back out and around again, almost unnoticed

the pulse thumps, groans echo and gurgle
low, hissing, deep in the body lost
in struggling labyrinths where consciousness

barely exists, mysterious
as immense spore systems, the ur-matter of mushrooms
underground, spreading for miles and miles

in earth's stomach, hot, dark,
waiting down there to be born, the pearly gauze
cobwebbed tissues feed delicately on each other

lip to lip, filament after filament opening
through the whole world until they pop up everywhere,
in forests, on lawns over old stumps rotting

under all our windows, toadlike, pure
venomous white or violent orange nipples,
each in its own shape, oddly

erect, familiar as babies but more powerful,
formed from the loam of what giant mouth
the veiled mucus splits open and then erupts

into totally new faces, abrupt gestures pushing their way up
from dark's seeming standstill out
into the light, sparks across the heavens shoot and then fall,

to the momentary eye seem to vanish
like seeds into night, movements that cannot, please
stay, I mean who's passing who,

which planet, are we at home
or not, the way mountains move
beneath our feet, on the trail looking upwards

at clouds rushing, flocks tearing across the sky
like the ragged galaxies wheeling
and spinning around our heads, whether you're stuck

stock still in the middle or swept along
in the dizzy current, minute
particles whipping through space, earth in its orbit speeds

like an open convertible with you, helpless, standing up in it,
at the prow of a ship with the wind, telephone poles, stars
streaming through your hair.

"But the strangest and most wonderful constructions . . . are the amazing, intricate constructions made by the primate, *Homo sapiens*. Each normal individual of this species makes a *self*. Out of its brain it spins a web of words and deeds, and, like the other creatures [spiders, birds, beavers, etc.] it doesn't have to know what it's doing; it just does it. . . . This 'web of discourses' . . . is as much a biological product as any of the other constructions to be found in the animal world."
—Daniel Dennett

WHIRLING DERVISHES II

> but even when you try to stop them,
> hold the kaleidoscope and its
> whirring fractions still so you can examine them,
> the carnival just keeps turning
> implacably onwards, of course you can't get outside, jump off
> the flashing gyroscope that keeps you alive
>
> except if you try spinning it yourself;
> whirl yourself around in place
> faster and faster, then slam, *stop!*
> abruptly, in your tracks
> out of the corner of your eye sometimes you can see it
> behind your back, on the periphery, what's
> always been there but hidden, like the Green Flash
> at the edge of the earth, just as the sun's coming up
> in the crack between two worlds, the lights
> of 14th Street just before you get to the station,
> the place at the tip of your tongue
> where the name you've forgotten hovers but where, where?
>
> —and then it arrives at 14th Street,
> "It's *George!*" you say,
> or *June,* or *Judy,* or *John:*
> how you managed it
> you don't know but you do it
> all the time; vault the gap between frames
> sometimes in a great painting
> for instance. of light that sees itself in shadow.
> or a piece of music. breathless, the high note
> and the lungs that sustain it, follow the surfer up
> to the crest of the wave and hold it

unbelievably, just as you suddenly find it
for yourself or perhaps in Shakespeare
or even the Bible, out of all those
figures in your head it's yours
to build on, the one blazing moment
that shocks you, hauls you up
by the bristling neck hairs into charged
dazzling recognitions that live
and never entirely leave you, especially when you say
what you thought you'd forgotten forever: say *14th Street,*
say *John.*
remember the Name.

IN BEAR COUNTRY

She has to write an essay.
Or a letter. Say "I need you"
and why. She reaches out for the words
and there they are, poof!
Like an ant trail, picking its way among bread crumbs
with a mind of its own?
Forget what the words refer to
or don't refer to. She inches herself
right along with them, over the sliding
talus slopes of the world.
Whenever she needs them they turn up
like stepping stones in the wilderness;
who put them there?
She thinks she chooses them carefully.
From pitons left on a rock face,
cairns full of dried berries.
But the minute she stops walking,
in the quiet after her own footsteps, hush!
What's that crackling
in the huckleberry bushes beside her? In bear country
she never stops talking, to warn the bears away.
But if all she can hear is herself what are the bears doing,
ahead, on the narrow trail
what if one of them should rise up
right in front of her with its hairy jaws open,
its raw, dish-faced snout
towering over her, and snarling?

Well, nothing. Is it all in her head?
For the moment. Still, what is this other
irritable static that starts up in her,

is it only the drizzling hiss
of extra-low frequency
intracellular transmission?
Like popcorn, filled with air and fast
or slow as lava. Woozy purple amoebae. Fat blueberries
with the silver lining of some storm clouds.
Or jellyfish. Floaters, she calls them. Almost intelligible
torn shreds of meaning. Not bears

really. But still frightening
to think about. Over the lost yips
of wolves, the pebbles grating underfoot
across the night, deep down
in her brain sky, is it only chemicals firing?
Sparklers splash the dark. In spicules of flaring light
they write their names on the air and disappear
even as she tries focusing on them, can't.
So she goes back to scribbling. In short stabs or in long
leaning sentences, thin snow fences shivering
"I want, I need . . . "
something. The bears are waiting;
what else can she do?
She'll never make it. But high in the mountains, on a white
empty snowfield, from the shifting valley floor
every once in awhile she can see them
far ahead of her, a tiny line of ragged
roped-together human figures
where there were none before.

THE GESTURES OF FEELING

But what does it *feel* like to be shot
on the screen in the middle of the living room?
Out on the digital highways
on the talk shows what mesmerizes
zips by on the surface. But even as cute beads of Jell-O
and Sprite bounce up and down in the vacuum
of virtual space, watch out,

                something's nudging at us
whenever we try to ignore it, attend only to words
clicking along like marbles, in the hypertext of the present
so many abstract options, so many unacceptable
secrets edited out, programmed
in living color for eyes only, naturally

                the rest of the body rises up:
in the smooth lagoon of the house with dangerous
clicking undercurrents, large sea animals prowl
that won't go away, like the reek of the smoking gun
ideas come from, what's that chewing at us but pain? Flashes of
last night's news:

                the bloody post office, the bank building,
and suddenly I think of my dead
friend Mary, out of her lovely mind
and perfect body she built a boy and a girl
who could have been astronauts, could have climbed
straight up out of her to the moon but then she exploded herself
with a shotgun in the master bedroom: now all the stories
I've ever heard open and close their fists
in my stomach and won't stop,

                    choppers shake the house
on their way to the next emergency, the animals want out
immediately, but sometimes they just want
to be stroked: how soothing it would be
if only they were made of nothing
but milk gurgling, vowels with puckered lips, juicy
and fat as plums but they're not;

                    try to forget them
and they grow teeth, tender bubbles of injury
like wounded walruses rise from computerized fish tanks
to explode in our faces, the slighted body breaks cover
and runs for it, out on the great glass
Monday night playing fields it almost makes it but I know lip gloss
when I hear it,

                  at the top of America's heap
and mine too, burning up the freeways
and swimming pools with them, the criminal's often hiding
in the back seat, I can't see him but how
could he have helped himself, undone
all those years, underneath all those expensive

                  shining surfaces, the hulking
shapes that come before words, that can turn
so easily into guided missiles, bloodthirsty
nasty cracks at friends. Even as we wash our hands
of front-page manslaughter, the shadows
that sleep inside us murmur

                    and crowd into the limelight:
unless we breathe on them, hold them in our arms
they'll tear up everything, they want
what all of us want, to be recognized but loved anyway,
to leap from the lids of our lives like dolphins, fuse all our inner
and outer selves into one broad
whale road for everyone;

                    sometimes just imagining it
it almost happens, something begins raining
in the throat, now every page
is wet with it, the greatest tales are lyrical
with the body's fluids, the limber
awkward bulk of a sea lion heaves itself up
into the living room but gently, side by side
with so many other thrusting

                    cerebral intimacies, animals
lumbering across the cortex, swinging
with sleek, lustrous thighs and other parts
of the muscular system,
with what visceral movements ideas back and fill
In. Out. Before. Behind. Above. Underneath
every utterance, in the deep spaces
and caves of the mind, thought knows itself and lives
in the motion of every corpuscle,

                    in the gestures of feeling that can shape us
into Homer's "sea shouldering whales," a phrase Keats imitated
whenever he said it, with huge, walloping shrugs

hunching his small shoulders to stuff
each syllable with the wet heft of flesh, the damp odor
of the wise animals we could be, alert to happiness
and pain too but seamless, peacefully lolling
with the welcoming hands of the waves we'd rule the world.

THE WORD FLOAT

And then the word float. The drift of it, turning
like an oboe, easily over the water.

O the relaxed circles.
Dazed glimmering spots

of sunlight on the motel's cool
chlorinated pool. Gold on the skin, the

tiniest hairs dusted. Also the nose, ears
and the shoulder blades, flattened-out wings

just resting on the world,
on its broad back.

Stretched out, soothed everywhere. In fluent
ribbons of lazy blue.

With easy yawns, sighs,
bikinis wallow beside us

like apples rolling in an orchard
of sweet balls, sweet bobbling breasts

and no need to say anything,
at least not yet.

Beyond, under the dry
rattling skies of America

cars rush between immense
sweeping wheatfields, lush

tall grasses lifting,
breathing under the wind

❦

as we would like to be, if we could only say it

forever and then live it,
the gold fuzz at the center

of a daisy is there simply, without any fuss
leaning where it is led

resistless, the tiny spokes of its wheel
small flags fluttering in the sun . . .

❦

So hands reach out to touch
what will not stay:

trailing its brief necklace of bubbles down
through all the green layers, in these velvety

dim currents the loud music of a passing
car radio dissolves, quickly muffled

❦

as imaginary fish wink
between our legs

as if this were the ocean, the casual cycles of desire

mounting upon themselves like waves,
gallons of them, cold, simple

and sweet as milk but speechless
as they were meant to be . . .

❦

Except for the soaring need
having imagined them, somehow

to articulate these vast shimmerings,
these undefined sheets wavering

across the land, in blurred lineaments flooding
over the cruel subdivisions, the sheer willfulness

of lives we can't help leading:

❦

because there is no love
possible without separation,

because there are black seedpods
sprinkled like pepper on the water,

in the core of the fruit, in the cradle

the distant speck of a bird grows
larger and larger, its radiance swings up

almost into a halo but then concentrates itself
into nickels, dimes, quarters:

tight as the buzz of flies

droning in the lobby,
mumbling over stale pop bottles

※

because there are trucks on the highways
and the need to name them,

because there are houses to be carried
from one state to another

speech struggles from the pool but dries up
as soon as it hits concrete.

As sentences squeeze out
sidewise, through cracked lips

everyone's mouth longs to open
all the way but dares not:

as the vowels harden, as the consonants click in

by nightfall only a few drops of water
glisten on closed skin.

THE LIFE OF EACH SEED

shrivels, hisses around our heads
as it joins all the rest. Dust sifts through our fingers
in Algerian cities, white buildings full of people
speaking French, sand sweeping into corners . . .
As withered pomegranates pile up in the market
in knobbed lumps, each embryo's sealed in its own jelly
so tight sometimes the questing tongue,
the puckered lips get tired
separating out each seed, in the living room's invented spaces,
The Silver Screen, The National Geographic,
the latest report from NOW on the coffee table
with bacteria like stars, rice grains stuck to the walls,
discrete bodies that loom through the skin of the tent . . .

As she opens to him, as he goes in to her,
lizards splay themselves in the weeds
next to the sidewalk, even in North America's backyards
and farther South, in patios
with broken bottles, geraniums
and pigs rooting, television antennae like steeples
in mountain villages stuck straight up
into the sluiceways, bands of featureless chatter
that wash overhead, the offscourings of objects
that never help, that rot in the mouths of nomads
and movie stars alike, as each extra in the crowd scene
imagines he/she is the one true fish
made to be multiplied, in his/her hand-me-down
never-to-be-equalled image, each snowflake or pearl

only to be reproduced, *Yes, Yes,* alike
but somehow different, can't you tell
the mother says, of her own
identical twins, *Buy now! Believe*
sometimes there really are miracles, tall, powerful
human beings who stand out, who tower over the city
like beacons, but it never lasts. Next day, in the heat,
the sweat of togetherness fouls everything with the stink
of anonymous increase: as pride teeters before the fall
in every subway, in broken sentences of stripped,
violently torn syntax kids hurl themselves against the walls
like slaughtered prisoners, the lives they leave behind them
in great scarlet letters of ragged Day Glo bleeding
the faceless graffiti of *No, No* . . .

LINKS / TALK SALAD / LINKS

And still the voices go on: this telephone
        is an international conference.
              Si, habla español. Third caller
    get off the line!
      CNN wants to talk to you,

each night it starts up
        like a motorcycle revving its engine,
    with so many conversations sniping at you,
           for now all you can do is lie back
      and listen to them, transparent
sentences forming and reforming

like Northern Lights, so many crackling
      modes of discourse
          in each one of us: wise,
lumpen, etcetera. Some stories
          you know well: half-heard
    body talk mumbles

below the threshold. In low
      squeaks. Grunts. *Pass the butter
motherfucker.* Slow dissolve into heavy
    biological landscapes. Sexually aroused turtles
        and thirsty lions.
    The need to use the toilet

only to come back to bed
      to more voices, authoritative
smart-alecky whispers. Puns. Labels.

        Sometimes even a skewed
     theory or two, viz.;

You sold the books, and the piano
         and that trout swimming over there in ink
    is a little surgeon, perfect grammarian of a man but who
        in her right mind said that?

Arrogant, self-assured
       as semioticians, *Vogue* models strutting,
    cracking their whips where you sputter
            like grease popping on a hot griddle, spitting out
    emptiness everywhere, *O Mish mash,*
      O Jargon, please

stop talking, suddenly you cry out:
       if nouns, verbs, hemlines
    exist for themselves only, what was it
    that time you went to a French movie and woke up
           next morning spouting French
    as you never could, in school
    or anywhere else,

what happened? Here in the shallows of speech
    which is your savior and throws you life jackets
        you gasp, come to the surface for air
      and almost sink again,
    but something's still swimming in you like a fish

you've never met: ecstatic
            as it is useful, the pure polyglot
        talk salad on your plate slowly shapes itself
    into huge fins rippling,
            the power of it surges
        into clever syllables weaving

and re-weaving themselves to invent
            bombs but also love letters
    and the urge to prayer: *O shadowy*
        trout of consciousness, surely the first link
in the long chain that delivers us is made of more than ink.

DOOR/WAYS

But what's on the other side could be
anything

doors with their wooden expressions
brand-new ones straight from the factory

leaning against each other like awkward
teenagers with their hands in their pockets

no paint no doorknobs
yet

doors suddenly gusting open
on loud voices

doors with the pursed lips of keyholes
in their faces

What they keep in
or out

presses against the stomach valve
and the mind lock and the churning

heart handle

one cell passes oxygen
from one membrane to another

hinge after smooth hinge

the door to the uterus the ear door
the door that keeps everything together

or apart I don't know

⁂

Once I had opened the front door
and the basement and the back door and the attic

I thought I was through but there are more plywood
barriers everywhere than there are seagulls in Boston

and more enemies, more swinging doors
to bang into than there are tears

in the harbor, salt that refuses to pour
because it's all stopped up, because there are so many stuck

doors to open / so many doors

⁂

Then I discovered *Webster's*
and the *OED*'s book of doors

in hushed libraries words
beckoning to each other like fingers

at the vaults of language fumbling
for the blessed click   the reward

in the body's brief stanza the poem
anxiously opening and closing

its eyelids those double doors

❦

"To know what is the meaning
of a passage first tell us

what it is not"

but if there are any definitions
that will contain water where are they

and why do we have to have them
for protection

❦

If the wind sees around
everything

would that help us to open them

the glass doors between life
and whatever comes next, dead

as a doornail

but still invisibly swimming
through all walls

      🙰

What if we broke through the skin
that sack of boiling juice

the magnificent sphincters / those sliding
oiled muscles inside

how could we stand the raw
dripping meat, the

unmentionable thoughts oozing
over love's cups

      🙰

And then there's the red, flashing
Exit sign at the movies

and the pantry door and the chopped-off
silent butler

broken into / at last

history's gates empty
mouths hanging ajar

⚘

The body may be soup
the body may be dessert

in the apple of the body
how many rooms should a poem have

and who should it talk to, inside
or outside

neither seems right

THESE WORDS

"Butterfly! These words
From my brush are not flowers,
Only their shadows."
—Soseki

        Reach out for one and it
        breaks off

        in the hand, the
        thin rice paper remains cling to you

        transparent,
        stick to the fingers but never

        solid, believable   as thick blood

        pounding up from the concrete
        pavement when you're jogging

        through the whole body   every ounce
        hot, steamy   close

        as the rest of the world
        isn't

        even as you grab   swallow
        or shove against it

        chains of thought wither
        away from you   like ashes

        from limp cigarettes   smouldering
        charred cylinders of paper

all by themselves   breathe on one

and it crumbles   only a smudge left
on the lips

all night pieces of them   jump up
like midges

between dreams, out of grass
you wish you were running through

quick as confetti, tiny
grains of alphabet   leap up

like insects   over your head
glints of light   flickering

specks, tiny parachutes

you can't get to, run
after them how you will

without pen or pencil

or net fine enough to collect
what refuses

to stay still but sometimes
just for a second   it happens

from locked drawers, all at once
petals swoop   like leaves

in gusts across the highway

flashing across fields
of disappearing   dew

uncatchable cells   ghost flowers

shape the vanishing trajectory
that is you

UNDER CYGNUS

It is all fire, fire and the reflections of fire;
long tendrils of flame looking at themselves and leaping
over water. In the moist tissues of the mind
we lie on our backs looking up
at the stars of the hippocampus.
The limbic system's
hidden messages scatter themselves through the cortex
like the Milky Way, *yes*. The thought strikes
like ice. The beauty of it. And the fear.
Lost, cold, disintegrating.
In field upon field of glittering
cloudy fire.

And yet we look like each other
and must say it: as the parallel motions of worlds
beyond the self shoot across the firmament,
hectic, quivering, fragile
as knots in a cosmic net,
each leap, each vanishing event
crackles like shrapnel;
in thin, fibrillating
hot gases, tangled proteins explode
from one neuron, one star cluster to another
as spidery webs light up
their flashing displays for brain scan
and satellite survey alike.

But why, how
do we reflect what? The outlines of nebulae ragged
as amoebae on a plate. Computer-generated
fractals. Or solar flares that erupt

every ten or eleven years. The not-so-random
limitless combinations of discrete
nucleotides in chains. Or the mind's shimmying
oscillations, its protoplasmic blurts
across the sky. Yes but with huge pits
in the center of some nuclei like the darkness
of dying stars. With even the live ones leaping
from synapse to synapse, in the mind's heavens hurtling
from cell to cell, with so many jittering holes
to fall into, where is the vanished One
we used to believe in?

For every positive
a negative. So crows call out to each other
from distant branches. Stars, pulsing and winking,
radio their lost light. And stones sit next to each other,
stranded. Here in my body, dim
uneasily valenced specks swirl
and cannot get out: though the imagery
tries to help, in this fantastic
journey through the intimate caves, vaulted
ribs, lungs, pelvic girdle, and bloodstream
that engulfs the skull and also circulates
far into space, who am I
really? Yesterday

I thought I knew, but the figure for it
keeps expanding, the universe
is ours and we are of it, interplanetary
flotsam, the dust of stars inside us

even as we ride through it,
beyond Jupiter speeding, farther and farther
and back again, what messages do we exchange
from then to now?
With nothing to hold onto
but the senses, a few bleached smells, fast-moving
blips, the dry sizzle of ozone,
whiffs of air incoming and then outgoing
in brief twinges, here in these eerily charged
decaying chambers there are no answers that are not
piecemeal, fragmented into the Many.
In shimmering strobic flashes, in the chasm between systole
and diastole I wake up gasping
in glittering ice-caves, tumbling across great voids

with no one to catch me but shapes
I make up myself, and they keep disappearing:
hatched out of endlessly complex
neat patches, braided sequences that click
and curl back on themselves, the scattered
birds of the mind are too many
and too restless. In May 1995
for instance, under the empty eye
of Cygnus, the Swan that leads us,
if the figures we follow are nothing
but pure wish, barely traceable constellations
that exist in the mind only, O most vacillating
tiny birdcages of protons, racing electrons,
neutrinos in their nuclei arranged
in streaks of absence, in fiery eruptions light-years

and nanoseconds away from where we were
and are no longer, who knows whether the darkness
is outer or inner?

So small, the things that go on in the brain.
And yet. How do we contain what we contain?
About to be shattered, swept up
across the sky in pieces,
we are what we are: exploding. Brilliant
as super novae. *Expanding even as we disintegrate*
in all directions, the shapes we imagine protect us
until we die: because of them no one dares
even to whisper we are not shining, not magnificent
as we are terrified, bits of blind membrane flying.

LOOK, IT'S POETRY!

I

At the office the new boss sniffs — O God
    she doesn't like us! Sizzle on the skin
        electric
   flushed griddle jittering — How infantile!
       the self says to the self,
    remembering the owly green
  Girl Scout spectacles, that playground
      where the girls gathered around us
    in a tight circle, in winter jackets poking
and jabbing at us, mean geese hissing *Fat! Fat!* —
Now, all grown up into contacts,
      into black kohl for eyeliner,
    we're still whining,
      still studying ourselves
in every poem wondering
   what strings us together, self
      and self-image and the words for it
   wavering in blurred glass —

Dearest Insatiable!
   No one adores you as I do.
The gentle shampoos on weekends, the sunny
   brisk, solicitous walks by the river —
but loving the buttery feel
    of your creamy cheeks I'm concerned;
      what was that twinge
  in our jaw when the woman winced, are we not all
   we appear to be, suddenly I'm choking

on our own tongue, now I am running our fingers through our hair
            tenderly, tenderly, what
       is that sick bird in our throat?

    The sting of consciousness pains us
            and that woman too,
      surely she meant no lasting harm but how
         profoundly our timbers shake
  at the slightest affront to it,
                the love for oneself one lives in
    like a foot in its shoe,
            she's calling the whole structure into question!
      Once the dialogue starts up
            it won't stop; bruises appear
      then calluses, toenails turn inwards
as words scratch at each other like ants, asking
        what does it mean to be messages
  in sealed bottles no one knows how to open?

As the salt cellar is full of itself so is the mountain.
        (But the salt cellar weeps when it's shaken.)
    In the dark mirrors of bars staring with such passion
    at ourselves, those two beautiful eyes,
  though we say all we want is love, someone else *with* us
      between the sheets, in the sudden delirious flash,
        the first thing we forget is the other;
          even the beloved's face
    blots itself out, where are you, I . . .
        and who's speaking, what . . .

As both lovers disappear,
        with every anxiety atomized
                into thin air, incandescent
as flames, the sharp white scent
        of a peeled tree trembling,
     in such unnameable fires there are no
possible distinctions left, but the molten core,
        the sweet flare of fusion
     sputters out almost at once:

Divided, smoke shreds itself into separate
        nerves, sinews unravelling, whispers
that start up all over again: talking to ourselves, arguing,
        frantically hissing,
            how will we ever know
    if we really *exist*, to others
as to ourselves, stuck behind spattered glass
      cloudy windshields cracked
by real sticks and stones,

With the Left Bank spitting on the Right,
        the woman at the next desk, each one
     glaring at the other, so frazzled
and terrified of it all we do
        is sharpen our tongues on each other,
          in clever territorial sorties
   we protect ourselves from *what*,
        what does that pinched face
pressed against the window *want*, which of us is speaking
           at any given moment: *Lines! Lines!*
    Why do we draw them so fine?

11

As the mountain is full of itself so is the salt cellar.
            (But the salt cellar pours itself out for others.)
     Sand runs through the hourglass
              gritty, unstoppable, fluid
       on the path by the brown river
            through fields full of wincing green
  traffic lights, weeds, flowers
         and tall trees turning their faces to the sky,

But some things belong to everyone:
             in the stunned spaces between us
   Look, it's Poetry!—
         bounding back and forth
             from one to the other like a giant
    golden retriever racing along the bank
              with her huge eyes, her big clumsy feet
   the lines she follows stretch everywhere
        and blur often,
     from delicate to punch drunk to soaring
           what she brings back to us is mixed
with what we send her out for, not objects
      but whatever holds us together,
   inside and then outside
         and back again, in spring air

Spiked with feathery lemon, the intellect's crisp mint
         in the barely distinguishable scent
   of smothered feelings released,

        beside the water dispersed, brilliantly flittering
    as dragonflies do, or mist
        like wisps of music ascending, careless of what it rubs against,
            the wings she holds in her mouth
      she barely breathes on: she knows she can't rescue

What's already dying, in long, tentative threads
            desperately stitched into bridges,
      with desire consuming itself, with forests
            dwindling into ashes,
    even as jet trails frazzle
          she keeps on going, shaggy
        as she is helplessly powerful, offering us
  words, images, slippers,
      everything conceivable to help us.

As the trees that protect us collapse
    she imagines furniture for us and we sit on it,
      beds to sleep on and we do, but now we are called civilized
we forget what brought us here, of course naming her
      Blue Ribbon, Best of Show
    but then ignoring her, looking out
        only for ourselves, the beloved bodies
we dote on, up to our collarbones in roast beef,
as the mirror ahead of us yawns open, no more reflections
        or even questions, at the end all we have taken
          eats itself out from under us,
    the soft edge of the path
  nearest the river slides, avalanches down into it
          like a sprawled body crumbling

III

But still Poetry pursues it,
        stumbling all over herself to retrieve
     what she knows she can never touch, only Bach
or Beethoven, or the last long drawn-out vowel
       of Mahler's *Das Lied von der Erde* vanishing
    into boom boxes, nor is it possible to escape
         like animals, or even trees,
eucalyptus with its rough
     silvery bark, "uttering joyous leaves"
without human companionship,
    the ache of consciousness that divides
   even as it sings to us:

As the gaunt stick woman clings
       to the child clutched to her ribs,
   whatever we believe in
is what takes care of us, back there on the playground,
on the Left Bank as on the Right, as the brown river deepens
      into salt everywhere,
into running and weeping wounds

As surely as language lies to us
    in the endless urge *to connect!*
        if the body were only the body, not torn
from one to the other, from the brooding pulp of flesh
    to the miracle it bears in its mouth,
what's left would be a wholeness
      monolithic as mountains, numb bottles filled

       up to their necks, with no salt free to pour out
but calm, perfectly untroubled
            by ourselves or anyone else,
     who would we speak to?
       Wordless
with silence ringing in our ears
            Listen! What would we hear?

III

BASKETS THAT HOLD NOTHING

"Without music, life would be an error."
—Friedrich Nietzsche

※

"Music brings to our daily lives an immediate encounter with a logic of sense other than that of reason. It is, precisely, the truest name we have for the logic at work in the springs of being. . . . at once cerebral in the highest degree . . . and at the same time . . . carnal, a searching out of resonances in our bodies at levels deeper than will or consciousness."
—George Steiner

※

"There is so much music in the world that it is reasonable to suppose that music, like language and possibly religion, is a species-specific trait of man."
—John Blacking

※

"I hear my being dance from ear to ear."
—Theodore Roethke

BEFORE DAWN

Cowbells in mist. Scooped, clotted
wooden coughs trail off into the distance.

Or church bells like empty bowls
tangled against each other in chains.

What lonely sounds
the mind makes, collecting itself.

Gongs clank, slow buckets
hauled by ignorant ropes climb up

on heavy copper footsteps over the lake,
then stumble away.

So we count the hours. To keep the flock
from straying.

The spaces between us are caves,

silences trembling like air
in the house of the cupped hand, the slight puff

of warmth on the skin as someone touches us
or just before:

One. Zero. Something
and its opposite.

In hollow chunks, mute
stones when the water dries up.

These lie around in the head
like birds in their feathers, or forks on the table sleeping . . .

And then the first A.

Vibrations ripple like a breeze
through the trees of the instruments. A green stain

rises up over the fields
at the first whiff of it, something about to be made

out of nothing.

For a moment the A only hovers
bodiless, on the threshold,

not swinging from raw
staggering hemp, or slung from the necks of animals

but tentative, feeling around in the underbrush
with invisible fingers asking

is this it, is this?

Then one note answers. And another.
And another after it, drifting from curtained wings

as the ropes slowly tighten.

On stage maybe only a single, brief
cry, or a low rustle in the bushes

as the fine, quivering
flutes nod to each other

and then begin:

delicately picking their way
along trails that know where they're going

because we invented them, gathered up bits
and pieces of meaning like kindling

for public bonfires, over every loudspeaker crackling,
language getting ready to pour itself

into longer and longer sentences, into cities
we thread together ourselves, with throbbing hammers poised

for the first strike, the sudden rush of air
around the clapper that creates it;

from the shapes of silences we feel
but cannot touch, sound

out of no sound, almost before we can stop it
let alone control it, civilization's astonishing

full orchestra comes roaring into the hush.

IN THE SKULL'S TINGLING AUDITORIUM

Tap. Step. Scuff, scuff down the hall.
            Or high heels clicking. The ears pick up the cue
    from Hush Puppies or even Birkenstocks,
            the mind showers you with sound bytes, laughter
        or love words, old stories, curses,
            each particular of the lifestyle
        and personality of the approaching presence . . .
Or sometimes it's music that does it. At the crash
        of a single chord often you know, exactly
            what's coming next, which fox-trot
    or Beethoven sonata, the recognition
        like a brisk cocktail waitress plants itself at the table
as rude as she is definite. *There*
            you are!

And the fragrance of it floods through you
        like attar of walnuts, long-ago templated rows
            you thought you'd forgotten fire off secret
        tiny glissades,
            passwords all at once remembered
    in rattling arpeggios, cool saxophone sprays tumbling
like silk scarves, there's no stopping them,

the limp popular tune
            that hangs on you like perfume. The sheer pour
                of a Lutheran hymn,
    once it begins, the ruthless
        indomitable intellect of the music,
            anthems that live themselves out
        in the history of a people, the remorseless
        unwinding structures, the entire giant being of it

      rises before you. The past surges into a future
irresistibly made flesh, but you have nothing to do with it
     or do you, how did it happen,
  in the skull's tingling auditorium
    each cell answers to what it's made for
  or teaches itself, helplessly leaping up into

waltzes. Kid's nursery rhymes. Lubricious
     torch songs, hands unbuttoning your clothes
  while you watch them, invisible keys unlock
    all your address books, telephone numbers, old cars . . .
   From the tinkle of a sixth-grade bicycle
to your father hacking in the bathroom, the cortex seems to light up

all by itself, where did *you* come from?
     you want to cry out but you can't,
  the crack of a baseball bat
   or the purr of a lover's voice, even the sneer
of an enemy, each makes sense of itself
    in sliding tissues, maps that mirror each other
   immediately in the muscles,

even listening to Mozart
    it's the same thing but more smoothly
  composed, the journey's variations prepared for
   carefully, as drums, flutes, horns come slipping
     or striding in their hiking boots,
  between forested strings the path
    winds among gray boulders, huge chords
   that seem to have been there always,
    waiting only to be struck

    to wake up humming, the silent architecture
        of the mind's concert hall engulfs you,
            the salt waters of the brain churn
    with bright electrical beads shimmering
      from scale to scale but the remembered salmon
        and wild rose of each summer

keep rearranging themselves, dispersed, twittering
    who knows where, into what
        aimless particles, disorderly
islands of entropy breaking down
each year into smaller atolls; if chaos is all we know
    no wonder music muffles itself in random
        abrupt patches of utter

  silence. In shrieks.
    In the steel scratches of despair dragged
          from pitch to pitch. Like mothers,
with stomachs convulsed we attend totally
        to the brown timbre of a cough.
    The tambourine skin and bones
of a smoky bar of blues. A question mark's
tag-end. A swearword's melancholy, long drawn-out
      drugged percussion.

But even hysteria's pizzicato
    stutterings among the japonica can't obliterate
        the patterns that came before, glimmering
    in plainsong or symphony,
in tango or march or lullaby,
    from the dense, sorrowful

        majestic lurch upward of the *Kyrie*
     in the Bach B Minor to the last rolling Amen,
millions of neurons crackle
        like forest fires over mountains

we can't control. For whatever enters the ears
     hides in us forever:
       the conflagration buries itself
  in the wet garden, Help!
          But you can't help it, eagerly
    the body lifts up its head
  at the blast of no matter what trumpet
     or whose forgotten voice
    ignites its balancing act:
       the ears' acrobatics inflame us to agitations
not our own, in delicate labyrinths jiggling
transparent hammocks of air vibrate to the motion
     of whatever still calls to us

in a folk song's minor insistence.
     In the blurred umbilical stream of the heartbeat
  of a mother's stomach that never stops muttering
    in the grown child's ear like a lover's whisper or a throaty
      sad violin lamenting
    the plain pity of it, in descending
      walnut boxes opening and closing
  some chord's always answering to tides
coming and going like the ocean, in taut strings rising and towering
       from a shoulder's sheltering bay into tall, foaming
  hollow waves crashing, then dying away . . .

BIRDS LIKE BASKETBALL PLAYERS

or string quartets talking back
                and forth to each other: question?
      answer: the violin says *Yes but*
          pass the ball!
and takes it away   runs with it
              liquid, quick-footed

as a flock of willets
         wily basketball players, feinting
     then dribbling the ball down the beach

the violin doesn't *look* at her teammates
              jostling behind her back
     but she knows where they are
exactly, tosses the melody right at
             one of them and he catches it
sometimes even   slows down

as in a beech grove   at twilight
         one bird   ?   answers another
      braiding and
    unbraiding
     with low, ringing
    wood-notes   drops of water
running, yes but in cluster
        after slow cluster

not territorial
        or for love only or even   hunger
     often just to go on

    play after sweet play
                between them

fingers tensed on a bow, claws
      on a branch
      hands on hard leather listening
            for the rasp of sneakers
      behind

only to repeat the
      same play but different
           deeper in the woods   more difficult
   wings scuffling to free themselves
        from dense, clutching   thickets

each new movement
      is a new idea, leaps
           swishes through the basket
   and back to the players, the
        strings pick it up

with slight variations   unfolding
           in soft triads, *Where are you?*
   the chestnut voices of phoebes
arguments, philosophies, faces

each extraordinary new species
      responds to what was said
         just before, curling
   from feather to neurotransmitter to eyelash

   elegant, classically determined
         the echoing caravans of whales
     around the world calling
  then answering each other

  or is it imitating, the
     plans of DNA
   the secret wiring comes
     from what molds, what shifting patterns
combining and recombining
     out on the court in the woods
    in concert
    in the mind

BECAUSE MY MOTHER WAS DEAF
SHE PLAYED THE PIANO

And golfed. Skied. Harangued the mild editors
of several newspapers. Like so many others, Hispanic
Chinese Haitian Indian Japanese
Italian mothers, in every language
obsessed, muttering angrily to themselves in parking lots
at rush hour, this particular one studied Russian

imagine, just to feel it
in her own throat, then make fun of it
embarrassed, because she was deaf
or because she was Irish, was that
bad? Ripped up the
celery. For the lamb chops, the boiled
potatoes for supper, who rang
                    the front doorbell? She'd run
Quick, into the closet,
turn the hearing aid down, tune out the loud, pithy
green kiwi fruit of the present with its too many
anxious blips, tiny beards in the salad, sure, why not

switch stations? From Marian Anderson to the great
Eleanor Roosevelt to Amy to Gertrude to Sylvia on the radio
my mother knew them all, but she liked piano best:
Bach, Mozart, Chopin and Scott Joplin too, also the Debussy
Petite Suite we'd play together
with me taking *Parte Secondo,* often after school
I'd come home and not find her, only Beethoven blasting
all over the house, then almost stumble over her

crouched, hidden behind the sofa
on all fours in front of the phonograph listening
with her whole body, she'd get right down there on the floor
on top of them, each undulating vibration, as even Beethoven
might have listened before her; first having plucked the notes
out of the upper and lower registers and then fiddled with them
so brilliantly, the remembered growl of the
bass clef or more delicate gymnastics, higher variations
he'd swing from so why not Mother?
                              She'd leap up all by herself,
flinging her tanned arms out
to Horowitz, Rubenstein, Dame Myra and Wanda,
even Art Tatum, sometimes she'd keep going
all afternoon until later, after supper
quieter. Washing the dishes, she'd wrap her cigarette tenor
gently around Billie. Judy. Or Edith Piaf or a Mexican
cradle song, slowly, with fires banked

when just that morning, in flames, she'd have been hatcheting at me
with pickaxes in the kitchen! No genteel
ladylike pecking order for her but outrage: after the scorched tendernesses
of the dutiful wife, in the fury of burned toast,
she couldn't help it, weeping and frantically shrieking
at everyone in her path, in between kisses
all her life patronized, scorned, ignored,
what else could she do?

              In the middle of America, alone
all day in the house with nothing but yesterday's
dirty laundry. With squadrons of button-down shirts
out there soiling themselves. Dragging socks from the
churning dryer, with only the washing machine's
dull thumps for company.
                    Most body language is dumb
they kept telling her, they tried to keep her quiet
but couldn't: what they forgot
was the ground under her feet, swaying in its chains
but still rolling, even as earth turns
from multitude to multitude, so many stilled voices,
trees fallen, mountains stripped and leveled
cannot be silenced forever:
                          for all she could not hear,
daily my mother laid down her body
for me and my sister, sputtering
Your father he . . . Who cares if they . . . Go, Move, Speak Up . . .
Make your own music or get out; no pre-ordained
hand-me-down hierarchies for her
or me either, her kid
from bassinet to grave, she lives in me like a crowd
of love songs and loud static,
                        because what's missing in our lives
is not cordless. Nor any kind of bodiless
information network; what she knew was touch,
velvet keys she pressed
tenderly, with pedals lumbering, just think of it,

                              my mother and maybe yours
pounding the ivories or not, with the same pulsing
up from the guts *obbligato* that's always changing
and never, Tallulah Bankhead, your huskiness
is ours. And Mae West, and Lauren Bacall.
Hoarse, throaty. Curling inside us like smoke
but so arrogant, passionate, peppery
everyone stops to listen to you,
                         nobody can shut you up
ever, my mother and I hear you with our toenails
the minute you open your mouths: *Hi, you*
I greet you and all the rest of you,
some say it makes no difference
in the long run, who says what
or how, but the body's dark
sheet music never stops tingling,
                         the ways we move are earthquakes
that won't go away: as every vibration shakes itself
into smaller and smaller fractions, as the vocal chords tremble
in sympathy with whatever lullaby
or struck tongue rouses us to wake up, step out to the beat

of the rhythm that's always there, waiting for the slightest
tap of a listening foot, ruffle of melody
in the ears, the quietest tune ribbons
all through us, which is why my mother is still waltzing
and playing the piano, from sleek suburb to farm,
from ghetto to desert city,

so what if she's gone, if the milk's long since dried up,
I'm still taking my shoes off
this spring, with the first pieces of pale grass
poking through hairless sidewalks because listen, friends,
whatever happens we're together,
                                  however altered
a few frogs still keep creaking,
the seas still shake with fish, the moon shrugs,
oil gushes from the mines, bread rises
against all odds: I only wish
my real mother were alive and could come too
but you'll do, you'll do.

CHASE SCENE, MANY LEVELS

Someone on the front steps, ahem.
Knock. Wait. But not for long, the
moment the conductor lets loose
the door opens on a windstorm, whole buildings blow away
like trees in a hurricane. Body and mind both
follow after them, from bargain basement to penthouse
kids squirt up and down the escalators

as everything swings into action.
Street people climb into window wells
dragging their cardboards behind them, bums wobble across
iron overpasses, cashmere
and silk business suits fidget outside elevators, Going Up?
Going Down? Sometimes it's hard to isolate

one movement from another, or one rhythm.
Or composer either. As sadness creeps up from the gutters
to listen in, to expand into great, swank
perfumed department stores, from floor to parallel floor
banked instruments sweep like boiling clouds
scudding across ceilings, voluminous
mountains of chords stack themselves up
in deep, vibrating piles. Intricate clicks and burbles

that talk back to each other and then stretch themselves, elastic
as saltwater taffy. Crowds of shoppers separate
into clusters of single notes, preoccupied faces ascend
from one escalator to the next, passing each other silently,
with embarrassed half smiles, but suddenly
as in a TV chase scene, a dashing cop

leaps over the guardrail, from the sleek Up trail
to the frantic Down trail or is it

the other way? The mezzanine hovers, superior.
Fountains of rosewater aspire
to the top floor like the long, windblown fingers
of fairy-tale cypresses. Outside, leaves fall
on scuffed shoes. Bronze arpeggios rattle
and then subside. Lazily. Into one or two scraps of paper,
kids lollygagging to school.

Or later, snow in the city.
Sheets of it slide across the streetlights. Friend
talks to friend on the telephone while the tongue probes
a piece of gristle from a tooth. Pulls at it. With a hollow
sucking sound, one of the friends whispers
something desperate, all the other noises
reorganize themselves, birds hop up and down the staff
to keep warm but the music changes again

in midstream, old memories open their arms
gently. On fire escapes for lovers
dangling their feet, on windy afternoons telling stories. Kites fluttering
and streaking above them. A woman on a stepladder changing
a lightbulb while the next-door neighbor peers down at her
from an upstairs window, what can possibly save us,
the spider tiptoeing up the wall?

Because what's coming now is rock climbers, teetering piccolos
like scared window washers holding on

with thinner and thinner fingers above the traffic.
As night rumbles below them, gnaws at their loosening ankles,
metal platforms hit bottom
in underground tunnels, shudder the entire city but not completely:
seagulls balancing themselves at the top
of barges dipping across the harbor lurch

and do not fall, pigeons shuttle upwards
like rugs rippling between buildings
as protein talks to protein, from pitch to quivering pitch,
calcium exchanges with potassium,
involuntary muscles stir, falling and then rising
like voices just out of earshot, there's no stopping them, each
snappy syncopation steps on the heels of the next

especially towards the end. The strings gather in the square
and then the bands, the massed, brassy crash
of tubas. Trombones. The street fills with them
as the legs jump up and run after them, trying to catch
whatever they can but there are too many extras,
too many kids bobbing in trees, too many sad
enemies and friends weeping, too many fiery conversations
and brave banners waving. Old soldiers salute

the last raising of the flag to the top of its staff
where it streams over their heads but finally it's unreachable,
there's so much going on, so much shimmering
and crackling in tiny corners, so much shine
from all directions, so many levels
everywhere in the mind.

COMPOSE YOURSELF

But still the woman keeps picking at it:
                      what does *think* mean?
    Or laugh, or shout, or weep?
                Like a cherry tree attacked by birds,
      hundreds of them, all jumping up and down
in concert but not quite,
                where did that speck go
            that just skittered past her eyebrow? She'd run
  after it but she can't,
              all she can do is keep circling
  in one place.

Because you can't encounter yourself
            in any mirror except reversed.
    To see her leaves turning look up
              through the mind's perches. Quivering net
    of sparkles, chirps, twitters.
                Notes sprinkled across a page
        as she watches,
    listens to the undersides of thought.

Flashing dissonances churn,
        tweedle around the brain stem. Up in one corner
  this happens, then that.
            At the same time, just below
    something else squawks, gurgles
        and then disappears.
      With loose ribbons of talk
            trailing after it, sounds meeting behind glass
    like chickadees at a feeder settling,

        then lifting away before she can say
Stay, explain yourselves; obviously it's up to her

whoever that is. She needs
            to figure this out but how?
      She takes the initiative
she thinks. She tries biology,
        shakes the tree of herself till the cherries wobble.
          Next she takes up logic,
    the crows of p and q teetering on a stepladder
she'd like to climb but it's too tricky,
        what makes anything stick
    to anything?

Back to the body again.
          But all she can hear is the ruckus
      of the usual traffic in her head. Occasionally
a clear argument comes along and she rides it
            as long as she can, the pure, purposeful
      arrow of a single idea.
  Please, let me go on
          says every endorphin,
              she hangs on to the theme
almost to the end but suddenly she jumps off, why?

Bubbles pop up around her.
           Unfolding like petals bursting, half-formed
    phrases bump into each other,
        the noises between her ears
make no sense, bizarre finches hide

                    among the leaves. The brusque hurry-up
of woodpeckers, irritable tympani tap their fingers
           to a rhythm she can't count, there's too much of it,
    too many things going on, *Compose yourself!*

her mother used to say.
        And so she does,
    or tries to, but how can she?
            In these waterless groves
      where are the springs of meaning
or who can measure them?
           Like an orchestra with no conductor
    she struggles after them without noticing
there's no need for it,
        the deep order she aches for
    is all around her,
arranging and rearranging itself in an orchard

she'll never understand except as music
        that sweeps over her, in the lush
    ripening lament of the bass line,
            the soaring swirl of an oboe
      she almost drowns but the strings come crying and flying
      in smooth phalanxes that lift her
    like waxwings swooping,
        flights of mind converging and then dissolving

only to return at once,
        in thin parallel sheets
           sister by sister rippling.

With red juicy trills
            and green skirmishes flourishing,
    in looped warbles
of excitement, long wavering bells, woodwinds tumbling
            and leaping in her head

untouchable, yes
    but *present*. As she is to herself,
                    given back to herself
        and beyond, moving with the music
            from dead center outwards
    released, sailing among the harmonies
            of so many different
    symphonic exchanges, ladders that hold her up
            even as they fall away:
        in music whatever comes
      immediately goes

but leaves itself behind.
        In the live, many-fibered codes
                of all orchards it's impossible
    but there she is, overlooking
            the multitude of herself like an orchestra
                in full bloom.
        In the bubble and chirrup of flutes,
            in the sweet, cellular mathematics
        of mind made manifest, she stops asking it:

what does *think* mean
  is a question with no roots
 and no milk to nourish her.
     Buried in each blossoming
 new movement, in each tiny
   spiraling cadenza or flowering
  swift sequence of notes like neurons firing,
    seeds weaving themselves
from generation to generation, in ringing
   petal after fleshy petal she's too deep
  in the next chorus to answer.

TREEHOUSE

When you're blind, when nothing touches you.
When nothing moves. When it's quiet.

Then a drop of rain. On a tin plate.
Roof of the house. Far off

in the big maple, *splat*. Tick.
From leaf to leaf

moving. Each flat
dusty drop squirts. Titters. Drips

down to the next level, so many
huge rooms, just

listen:
anvil to stirrup to hammer

your chest fills,
the outside rushes in.

Especially when it's not rain
but Bach, maybe,

quick, in the woods, then slower,
tall columns of sound beckoning you

deeper and deeper, each voice calling
back and forth to the others, what are these

spaces opening out for you, round
hollows you can step into

smoothly, clearings where you can move out
from the rumbling laps of chords

and between them. Surrounded by redwood trunks,
trails winding through the forest

༈

go on. Follow them. You can.
With yawns, deep breaths

from the top of the brain to the bottom.
Nerve cells

all over the body branch out, perception
piles itself on perception.

Up behind the temples
piccolos, little pieces of thought jump

from twig to twig, yes
you can hear yourself think, in music

༈

in rich, twanging vibrations
strings gossip, from the basses

the constant grumble of desire. Above,
from the sonorous right half

of the cortex to the clever syntax of the left
or vice versa, ideas ricochet

off each other, now you hear them
now you don't, though they say

the distance between low C
and middle C on the piano

is almost the same as the interval between the two areas
that hear them in your brain. Soft sounds light up

some rooms. Loud sounds spotlight
others, upstairs and downstairs

strobes crackle and hiss, so many
levels of illumination, *flash*

your mother frowns at you from the kitchen,
whispers leap up and die down

all over the house. With old wives' tales
dismembered. Long-ago snatches of song,

marching orders, smart footsteps like snare drums
break up and then regroup

like gulls quarreling. Whole paragraphs
of new information, facts rush in and out

⁂

from room to room expanding
like steam in rusty radiators.

With sighs, creaks, groans,
startled exclamation marks rising

right up to the attic, in the terrified moral ping
of cold air heating up

like shrill tendrils,
torn cobwebs tug at you

in the middle of a long speech
you're trying to make to yourself in the study

⁂

Wait! somebody interrupts
in another rhythm entirely

Be quiet, you tell yourself,
but the heckler's raspberry erupts, rude sounds

sputter in the background. With coughs. Harrumphs. Dark
horizontal streams rustling on top of each other like branches

that keep quivering, in tiny accidental
puns, wordplay, screeches

like chalk on a blackboard, crossed
fingers for luck but not wires:

꽃

blind, you can still move
to the sounds you hear, with great sweeping wings

from the cellos, from shuddering rosewood,
from walnut cornucopias spilling

even in the busiest
cerebral foliage, in dense

polyphonic crowds murmuring there are still paths,
cadences to lead you onward

꽃

from one scale to another, quiet
but still moving. From the faded keys of the past

to the brisk fruit of resolutions
you know will be coming soon

or not coming. But even with so many dissonances
dissolving from limb to limb

the future is still hovering ahead of you
where it always was:

in the deep, rainy
live present of leaves

in the mind's forest glimmering
there, where you're moving towards it

faster and faster now, perhaps whistling a tune
to keep yourself company?

BASKETS THAT HOLD NOTHING

Mind like wickerwork, crisscrossed
              baskets that hold nothing, gatherings
        that almost but not quite come together.
Though they may have, in the beginning,
            with each side of the gap
      in the tender skull knitting itself to the other,
   what governments, what grand cathedrals we have made
        and then abandoned:
           now, in Shea Stadium
        wind brushes yesterday's pennants
              around the field in tatters.
    Forgotten faces nod
        through the gaps in all our sentences
  but won't go away completely:
      with no more *thwack* of the bat
            or fish in the river, in autumn no more shimmering
   loops of nylon or *whap!* caught the ball,
        though tangerine leaves, brown speckled,
     rush headlong at each other
  and then apart, without touching,
each spring you can hear it
        out on the green diamonds
    and icy streambeds, once more shouts of pleasure
        as each new hatch rises,
    over and over the click
           and stubborn whirr of reels
   of players who won't go home:
           in a blur of insects spinning
they keep after it, to the disappearing *slap*
   of fish surfacing,

      at the outermost edges of the eye
     their long lazy lines stretch out into space,
their delicate networks intricate
       as music, almost invisible
    with nothing in it?
      O absolute elegance of Shape.

FROM THE CLIFFS

Church bells again, at Easter.
Old. Plonking. Talking to each other
all around the lake in clumsy
odd blurts, rough
timid voices that speak to each other,
then pause . . .

Like smoke from morning chimneys.
Doves in gutters, cavernous
iron wheels dying away only to start up
all at once, sweet, cracked
plates of sound step out over the water . . .

but the listener does not stir.
Sitting on a stone bench
in half drizzle, half sunshine
high over the lake she names the notes to herself,
then plays them

on the piano in her head
as if they'd been there all along. In different
combinations. Chord,
discord. Shoving each other with soft
falling-away cries.

Raucous, then gone. Out there in the mist,
the disappearing churches, the gray bell towers'
shivering stone ribs. But inside, each tiny
quivering harmonic keeps climbing
higher and higher in her chest. Reaching
from one note to the next, invisible

as the feelings in her half-sleeping, half-waking
blue-jeaned left leg,
swarms of insects prickle
from ankle to thigh, buzz
but eventually dwindle away

as the bells begin again:
beyond the nubbled pink
nylon parka she zips closer to her, everywhere
sounds she did not make tremble
on violet wings muffled
into spectral rainbows,
pale ladders stretched over the lake

and shredding themselves into pieces,
diminishments that will not leave her,
so secret they are,
and deep. The hairtrigger cells stored
in the church of the ears wait only to wake up
to divide themselves into fractions,
infinite ripples that reach out
farther and farther, on whose shore do they end?

The bells keep asking for something, but slower
and slower.
The listener sighs. Shifts
the lake inside her from one leg
to the other. Beads from last night's rain
hang from fence wires strung taut

in front of her face. Nothing but steel blue
icy lake water behind them. Far below, merciless
steep waves.

But now birds begin to look for each other
in the intervals: C? E? G?
A rattle of ravens
veers up, almost collides with her
before they wheel away.

Nearer, the reedy click
and wheedle of smaller birds,
bright holly berries in the bushes.
Or ducks squawking, sleek, green-ringed
streaking across the sky
with car horns in the distance,
boats cutting their motors.

As the gaps between notes spread out
the listener keeps waiting for it, inside
or is it outside? Sound
is the last sense to leave us.
The listener looks down from above
at the backs of seagulls swooping
silently, over the water.

DIRECTING CHAPULTEPEC CASTLE

(in Beethoven's Fifth; the Mexico City Performance)

I

Conduct a castle? Ridiculous. But there she is:
    with Beethoven in her earphones
        opposite Chapultepec Park and eye level
with the castle itself, on the hospital's sixth floor
    stranded, stuck in her paper shift and barefoot
        beside the bed, she's back from the bloodletting at last:
waving her pretend baton at the picture window and wobbling
    like a white-sheeted candy skeleton, it's the music
        that enters her now: when she tells the castle
move, the castle moves. Its giant stones
    plunge downwards and then raise themselves with the kettledrums
        surging upwards, with a flourish of her magic wand
its battlements turn into strings, woodwinds, brass
    heaving inside her,
        each royal instrument and flaring nerve end
deep in its casement quivers,
    in live, mullioned windows, in every cell blazing,
        bone structure and building too
like sand solidified, that shifts and does not shift.
    For the menace of it will not be put down
        nor the majesty either:
though it's not even a symphony
    she particularly likes, repetitious
        and slightly boring, it invades her
like a conquering army, she protests
    but can't stop them, vast
        grim-faced boulders

hauled from the valley below. The tall, shrieking
    turrets of jagged horns. Slabbed
        iron chords at the door, gates that almost close
but barely; see, there's a loophole
    and she's pointing at it,
        massed forces break into pieces and disperse
into shimmering triplets cascading, the castle seems to sigh
    and she with it, released.
        Into brief showers. Into apricot gray courtyards.
Into closes and quiet keeps
    where children play, attentive
        to old murmurings in the cracks, mossy
winds from nowhere. In the bare, antiseptic cold
    of the room around her, the sheaths of her muscles gingerly
        loosen. Stretch themselves into one long
narrow ribbon the oboe picks up and streams out
    over the castle's forehead like a brook in winter,
        like a lone hawk circling
until Beethoven catches it
    or she does, since it's inside her.
        But soon enough it starts up
all over again, she's engulfed
    once more by the horror, the flooding fear
        of what comes next: in the strident
jolt of pain in the gut, the biting worry
    over torn stitches, the entire symphony folds itself
        into Beethoven's churning troughs as she sinks
almost to the bottom. In her bare feet, with her beloved
    enemy body she's beaten,
        obliterated by the crunch of tanks,

the shattering nasal roar
    of triplets finally flattened into the crash
        of mailed fist rapping on shuddering door.

11

Which still stands, which will not give in because listen,
    what comes next is a nurse with a glass of chamomile.
        In the fragrant hands of hope
lifting itself from the basement, throbbing baritone
    waves of sweeping cellos press upwards
        in smooth, bottle green tides slowly rising
like warm syrup, like bread, O comfort, welcome
    she hums beneath her breastbone, softly rocking
        in such soothing currents she thinks the pain will let up
and so it does, but returns
    almost immediately, each theme dissolves
        into the next only to come back
a few bars later, but repetition
    with variation is life, she tells herself, full of
        surprises! And now the fierce pleasure of it
sizzles in her ears as the tempo quickens into thousands
    of slim bicycles pumping,
        Beethoven's fireworks spill out over the boulevard
spread below her.
    In taxis. Checkered umbrellas.
        People crossing to the Park. With beggars. Tortilla vendors
and pet dogs. Underbrush climbs the hill
    through tossing boughs to the stone skirts of the palace
        riding above them, on heaving swells of ocean
she and the castle are boats rising and falling

     in patchy sunlight, with a light rain in the fiddles
         and those ancient breezes.
Whenever she gives the cue
     the trumpets' brazen spears, the woodwinds mute themselves, slipping
        and sliding through long halls
where faded tapestries rustle, where intricate neural draperies
     ripple against the walls with the same alternating strengths
        and weaknesses as before. Always the great bronze
clang of footsteps. The boom of surf against rock
     which she will resist:
        not by standing still but by moving
inside her body to the music's muscular rhythms,
     the damp organs flushing, in and out
        in secret combinations only she
and Beethoven know, which is how they conduct each other:
     as the royal banner hitches upwards
        on its hollow staff, interval by straining interval
it leaps to the top, like fluid in a heated tube
     or a globule of lymph, an isolated eighth note of protein
        that gracefully meets another, in the fluent
braided duet of two birds now, in precise
     sweetly doubled flight
        flute and clarinet come soaring
high over the chained orchestra
     till they almost escape, but the surf
        rises against them:
though they seem to make it to dry land, in the tiny
     tweedling *oompah-pah* of a band of strolling dwarfs
        she knows it won't be for long; since this is Beethoven

nobody's going anywhere,
    once more the power of bodies to be crushed
        is too pitiable, too heart wrenching. And strong.

III & IV

But now the horses come running, running
    straight up against the window,
        between her and the castle they pour
from the sad campo flying
    in dusty whirlwinds, packs of neighing molecules,
        hooves, nostrils, tails in a roiling stampede
of huge silky haunches that halt
    instantly, at the gold blast
        of the triplets again, this time it's the trumpets
that shout, goose-step across the courtyard
    till it shakes beneath her,
        deep in her bowels, in stone dungeons
the basses lunge upwards with the mares, stallions
    galloping over the drawbridge, weaving through cold corridors
        like shots of adrenalin, their hearts beat
faster and faster, but all at once they stumble
    into somber polkas, thick woolen hooves
        heavily syncopated. Weird as any wheedling
circus ponies. In single file plucked
    for princes and princesses
        or who is it? In the Great Hall
collared dragons growl
    and strain at the leash, some
        sinister birdcall beckons,

a clarinet cries out loudly
    as the sky darkens, thunderous
        clouds begin to grumble
what is it,
    what's coming next,
        and suddenly it blurts out

---

the whole seething ball of it, the sun! And she's holding it
    in her two hands.
        Arms, legs outstretched
to the four points of the compass, North South East West
    leading the orchestra she's the center
        of everything: stick figure filled with the music
of her own body, these flames, this solar burning
    is all she'll ever know
        or need to, in this hotbed consuming herself
first slowly, then faster,
    tottering still but with bold
        regal arms swooping,
lurching on shaky limbs
    with storms to the right of her hissing
        at storms to the left of her banging
she lifts her head to it, the wild, keening
    voice of the Rider within her.
        Caught in this wordless surge
of milling animals, in the low, choppy wash
    of phrase talking back to phrase, she corrals all of them,
        sweeps them up and then joins them

at the highest crescendo of pure, tossing pain
    she gathers her forces; at first rough,
        trampling across the moat
but then smoothly, the violin's velvet legato
    pours over her and whips upwards
        enormous, answering the icy echoes
of clanging cymbals, white-maned
    mountain ranges looming beyond the castle,
        raising their flashing shields
all around her, swinging her whole body
    in great, rubbery circles,
        then straightening herself on the ramparts,
out of the crosswinds at last. As sweetness
    that only whispered to power now joins it
        one, two, three, there's a regiment
of utter joy inside her, the instruments in her blood
    canter through her veins like brother and sister
        sleek racehorses rippling,
taking whatever comes
    and then riding off with it, in bruised
        tender flesh whose strength will not be put down
nor weakness either:
    even as twanging chords
        like battering rams shove at the fortifications
there are light winds playing above them,
    strings like wild strawberries waltzing
        and far-off horns. That lead her
out the window, beyond even the palace
    to the glittering horizon, the lid about to bang shut
        except for the sudden fanfare

of the triplets again!
    Three loud blasts
        shudder the castle but this time she refuses
to cower beneath them, this time
    the Rider in her nightgown gives up,
        throws even the conducting away.
In a wild rush of hooves, bugles, uncontrollable
    animals charging the gates, snorting
        and running, running, right to the edge of the cliff,
the Rider gathers her robes and hurls herself
    into the pit of the volcano,
        and there finds herself
stopped dead. Broken, but still breathing.
    And picks herself up:
        under the pound, crash, thud
of the music's final footsteps she's relieved,
    oddly relaxed. Holding herself close
        in her own arms, she knows she and the castle
are motionless but full of movement:
    with the reins clenched in her fingers
        she climbs the roaring sides
of the heaving symphony and disappears with it
    into the distance, trailing streamers of smoke
        high over the hospital
and the whole city, brandishing
    against the lowering sky one white-knuckled, triumphant
        trembling fist.

LIFELINE

Finally, so many statements
and restatements. Child with its grandmother's

quick step and then stumble. Theme and
variation done to the ground.

Over and over. Braided
strand upon strand. And the pain of it,

the harsh, bullying anxieties of ordinary
life hurrying to a coda,

an end you'll never know but listen:

the sound's only a question mark
when we first hear it, the shy opening notes

delicate as a cat's paw curling
under a door but lengthening, lengthening . . .

Thread of melody to hold onto.

The long single line lays itself out
like honey for us to follow, it spoons us under arches

and into old temples, nests where we can rest for awhile

and stop fretting. Attend only to the low
breathy purr of it, the clarinet's liquid mutter

soft. Gentle. Thin as an owl by daylight

that wants us to look out the window
and recognize ourselves, ambling

by the banks of a river. Lazy

as summer sprinklers. The green smell
of water talking to itself

or saplings in a breeze. A spindly
white birch tree like a dancer

barely visible, a great beauty

at the end of her swan neck examining herself in the mirror
first this way, then that way . . .

Until the piano joins in, crash

and the water doubles itself, the mind explodes
into clever fractions, cells interrogating each other

in fine flashing sheets,
transparent patterns shifting,

picking up speed, flickering
in the yes-and-no keys of an express train,

what train? The music gives us its windows

in little scenes whipping by
from Boston to New York and back again,

Presto. Allegretto. Scherzo. Puckers our mouths up

in a surprised whistle exhaling
what, is it really possible to get somewhere

in shapes that are no shapes but changing?

As the tempo quickens, as the weight that is no weight
bears down on you like the future about to be born,

in the quick coupling and uncoupling
of flesh, phrase, *idea*,

for awhile even a donkey's cry, even the raw meat
of agony may not matter

as long as they keep answering each other
in the same key, the two instruments moving

each on its own trajectory but together,

in parallel operating theaters like intelligent
piano-faced doctors conversing

with their crisp chords, their black-and-white sticks of advice

accompanying you until you arrive, gasping
at what entirely new place?

Da capo al fine.

Washed. Clean. Shaken. But soothed also,
the clarinet stands on one leg

looking at itself in the water.

Barely moving but various
as thought collecting itself

it murmurs among deep pools, many-colored scarves from India
by way of Boston, why not?

The mind holds hands with itself in music

and beyond, wherever it began
larger now, in clear ripples streaming

supple as heavy silk
or darker, in thick scoops of maple

each separate note hangs on the lip of the last
and then folds over, in slow

amber peninsulas stretching out

like a dancer's arm extended, high overhead reaching
and then collapsing, shoulder to elbow to wrist

in great shining bolts of ribbon unspooling

seamless. With nothing left but echoes,
memories rustling through it

like wind through a pipe: the long sweet wavering of it
vanished but not quite.

ACKNOWLEDGMENTS

I cannot conclude this book without expressing my gratitude to its first readers. For responses ranging from interlinear markings to overall assessments, from answers to particular questions to challenging critical readings, I thank everyone who has ever commented on these poems, but especially Cal Bedient, Philip Booth, Debi Kang Dean, Jonathan Holden, Carolyn Kizer, Mark Levine, Marlon Ohnesorge-Fick, Bob Phillips, Patricia Traxler, Helen Vendler, John Wolff, and my two Milkweed editors: Emilie Buchwald first (she of the perfect pitch), and also the super-perspicacious Molly McQuade. Nearer home there are others I must mention; first of all Connie Poten, incredibly sensitive and astute critic, unflaggingly generous friend. Caroline Patterson "lent me her musical ear" at just the right moment. And finally, besides the always helpful comments of the eight other members of the Rattlesnake Ladies Salon—Sandra Alcosser, Sharon Barrett, Kate Gadbow, Dee McNamer, Megan McNamer, Marnie Prange, and Jocelyn Siler—there are the unfailingly wise counsels of my husband, Leonard Wallace Robinson, under the sign of whose love these words were written.

My thanks also to the editors of the journals in which the following poems, some of which have since been revised and/or retitled, first appeared.

American Literary Review: "As In a Cage"
Beloit Poetry Journal: "In These Burning Stables," "The Jelly Between the Ears," "Ten Billion Blackbirds," "In Bear Country," and "Before Dawn"
Controlled Burn: "Directing Chapultepec Castle"
Cream City Review: "On the Porch"
Cutbank: "Ideas" and "Because We Are Not Separate"
The Georgia Review: "For Wiley, Age Six Months"
Hubbub: "These Words"
The Hudson Review: "Stream"
The Kenyon Review: "Stop the World"
The Manhattan Review: "The Gestures of Feeling," "The Word Float," "Under Cygnus," "In the Skull's Tingling Auditorium," "Chase Scene, Many Levels," "From the Cliffs," and "Lifeline"
The New England Review: "Look, It's Poetry!"
New Millennium Writings: "Precious Bodily Fluids"
The North Dakota Review: "The Three Tortoise Secret-of-the-World Power Plant" and "Danger of Falling"
Ploughshares: "What the Skin Knows" and "Cousins"
Poet Lore: "Birds Like Basketball Players"

Poetry Northwest: "Treehouse"
Prairie Schooner: "Because My Mother Was Deaf She Played The Piano"
The Southern Review: "The Life of Each Seed"
Switched-On Gutenberg: "Whirling Dervishes II"
Three Rivers Poetry Review: "In This Landscape"
The New Virginia Review: "Uncharted"
Willow Springs: "Wild Card"

I would like to acknowledge the following works, to which, among many others not cited, I am indebted not only for some of the ideas, but also for some of the neurophysiological backgrounds against which many of the poems are set:

Leonard Bernstein, *The Unanswered Question: Six Talks at Harvard* (Cambridge Mass.: Harvard University Press, 1976).
Colin Blakemore, *The Mind Machine* (London: BBC Books, 1988; revised edition, London: Penguin, 1994).
Stanley Burnshaw, *The Seamless Web: Language-Thinking, Creative-Knowledge, Art-Experience* (New York: George Braziller, 1970).
William Calvin, *The Cerebral Symphony: Seashore Reflections on the Structure of Consciousness* (New York: Bantam Books, 1989).
Francis Crick, *The Astonishing Hypothesis: The Scientific Search for the Soul* (Maxwell, Canada: Scribner and Maxwell International, 1994).
Richard E. Cytowic, *The Man Who Tasted Shapes* (New York: Putnam, 1993).
Daniel Dennett, *Consciousness Explained* (Boston: Little, Brown & Co., 1991).
Gerald M. Edelman, *Bright Air, Brilliant Fire: On the Matter of the Mind* (New York: Basic Books, 1992).
James Gleick, *Chaos: Making a New Science* (New York: Viking, 1987).
James Gleick, *Genius: The Life and Science of Richard Feynman* (New York: Pantheon Books, 1992).
Steven Pinker, *The Language Instinct* (New York: William Morrow, 1994).
Steven Rose, *The Making of Memory* (New York: Bantam Press, 1992).
Oliver W. Sacks, *A Leg to Stand On* (New York: Summit Books, 1984).
Oliver W. Sacks, *The Man Who Mistook His Wife for a Hat and Other Clinical Tales* (New York: Summit Books, 1985).
John R. Searle, *Minds, Brains, and Science* (Cambridge, Mass.: Harvard University Press, 1984).
George Steiner, *Real Presences* (Chicago: University of Chicago Press, 1989).
Anthony Storr, *Music and the Mind* (New York: Free Press, 1992).

And finally, I am deeply indebted to the Rockefeller Foundation for an Artist's Residency at its Villa Serbelloni in Bellagio, Italy, during which a great deal of the work on this book was accomplished.

The epigraphs in this book are from the following sources:

John Blacking, *How Musical is Man?* (London: Faber and Faber, 1976), 7.
Daniel Dennett, *Consciousness Explained* (Boston: Little, Brown & Co., 1991), 108, 416.
Gerald Edelman, quoted in Steven Levy, "Dr. Edelman's Brain," *New Yorker*, 2 May 1994, 62–73.
Albert Einstein, cited by J. Hadamard, *The Psychology of Invention in the Mathematical Field* (Princeton, N.J.: Princeton University Press, 1945).
James Gleick, *Genius: The Life and Science of Richard Feynman* (New York: Pantheon Books, 1992), 131.
David Hume, quoted in Daniel Dennett, *Consciousness Explained* (Boston: Little, Brown & Co., 1991), 412.
Friedrich Nietzsche, quoted in Anthony Storr, *Music and the Mind* (New York: Free Press, 1992), 163.
Friedrich Nietzsche, quoted in Elliot Ravetz, "The Melodies of Nietzsche," *Time*, 24 April 1995, 74.
Rainer Maria Rilke, *The Selected Poetry of Rainer Maria Rilke*, ed. and trans. Stephen Mitchell (New York: Vintage International, 1982), 316.
Theodore Roethke, "The Waking" in *The Collected Poems of Theodore Roethke* (Garden City, N.Y.: Doubleday and Co., 1966), 108.
Soseki, quoted in Stewart W. Holmes and Chimyo Horioka, *Zen Art for Meditation* (Rutland, Vt.: Charles Tuttle & Co., 1973), 90. Haiku trans. Yasuko Horioka.
George Steiner, *Real Presences* (Chicago: University of Chicago Press, 1989), 218.

Patricia Goedicke is the author of ten earlier collections of poetry and has received several national grants and awards for her poetry, including a National Endowment for the Arts Fellowship. In 1991 she received the University of Montana's Distinguished Scholar Award for creative activity, and in March through April, 1993, she studied at the Bellagio Study and Conference Center on Lake Como, Italy, after being awarded a Rockefeller Foundation Artist's Residency.

Educated at Middlebury College and Ohio University, Ms. Goedicke has taught poetry at Hunter College, Sarah Lawrence College, Ohio University, and the Instituto Allende of the University of Guanajuato in San Miguel de Allende, Mexico. Currently she teaches in the University of Montana's Creative Writing Program in Missoula, Montana, where she lives with her husband, Leonard Robinson.

Interior design by Tree Swenson

Typeset in Sabon

by Stanton Publication Services, Inc.

Printed on acid-free Booktext Natural paper

by Bookcrafters

MORE POETRY FROM MILKWEED EDITIONS:

Passages North Anthology: A Decade of Good Writing
Edited by Elinor Benedict

Civil Blood
Jill Breckenridge

Drive, They Said: Poems about Americans and Their Cars
Edited by Kurt Brown

Astonishing World: Selected Poems of Ángel González
Translated from the Spanish
by Steven Ford Brown

Mixed Voices: Contemporary Poems about Music
Edited by Emilie Buchwald and Ruth Roston

*The Poet Dreaming in the Artist's House:
Contemporary Poems about the Visual Arts*
Edited by Emilie Buchwald and Ruth Roston

*This Sporting Life:
Contemporary American Poems about Sports and Games*
Edited by Emilie Buchwald and Ruth Roston

Windy Tuesday Nights
Poems by Ralph Burns
Photographs by Roger Pfingston

The Color of Mesabi Bones
John Caddy

Eating the Sting
John Caddy

The Phoenix Gone, The Terrace Empty
Marilyn Chin

The Man with Red Suspenders
Philip Dacey

Twin Sons of Different Mirrors
Jack Driscoll and Bill Meissner

Mouth to Mouth: Twelve Mexican Women Poets
Edited by Forrest Gander

One Age in a Dream
Diane Glancy

Paul Bunyan's Bearskin
Patricia Goedicke

The Tongues We Speak
Patricia Goedicke

Sacred Hearts
Phebe Hanson

The Art of Writing: Lu Chi's Wen Fu
Translated from the Chinese
by Sam Hamill

In a Sheep's Eye, Darling
Margaret Hasse

Trusting Your Life to Water and Eternity: Twenty Poems by Olav H. Hauge
Translated from the Norwegian
by Robert Bly

Boxelder Bug Variations
Bill Holm

The Dead Get By with Everything
Bill Holm

This Error is the Sign of Love
Lewis Hyde

Looking for Home: Women Writing about Exile
Edited by Deborah Keenan and Roseann Lloyd

The Freedom of History
Jim Moore

The Long Experience of Love
Jim Moore

Minnesota Writes: Poetry
Edited by Jim Moore and Cary Waterman

The House in the Sand: Prose Poems by Pablo Neruda
Translated from the Spanish
by Dennis Maloney and Clark Zlotchew

Earth Tongues
Joe Paddock

Sweet Ones
Len Roberts

Firekeeper
Pattiann Rogers

Forgiveness
Dennis Sampson

Clay and Star: Contemporary Bulgarian Poets
Translated and edited
by Lisa Sapinkopf and Georgi Belev

White Flash/Black Rain: Women of Japan Relive the Bomb
Edited by Lequita Vance-Watkins and
Aratani Mariko